Dean Peer's Bass Harmonics

NEW CONCEPTS AND TECHNIQUES

Project Manager: Colgan Bryan
Cover Design and Art Layout: Joann Carrera

WARNER BROS. PUBLICATIONS - THE GLOBAL LEADER IN PRINT
USA: 15800 NW 48th Avenue, Miami, FL 33014

WARNER/CHAPPELL MUSIC
CANADA: 40 SHEPPARD AVE. WEST, SUITE 800 TORONTO, ONTARIO, M2N 6K9
SCANDINAVIA: P.O. BOX 533, VENDEVAGEN 85 B S-182 15, DANDERYD, SWEDEN
AUSTRALIA: P.O. BOX 353 3 TALAVERA ROAD, NORTH RYDE N.S.W. 2113

NUOVA CARISCH
ITALY: VIA CAMPANIA, 12 20098 S. GIULIANO MILANESE (MI) ZONA INDUSTRIALE SESTO ULTERIANO
SPAIN: MAGALLANES, 25 28015 MADRID
FRANCE: 20, RUE DE LA VILLE-L'EVEQUE, 75008 PARIS

INTERNATIONAL MUSIC PUBLICATIONS LIMITED
ENGLAND: GRIFFIN HOUSE, 161 HAMMERSMITH ROAD, LONDON W6 8BS
GERMANY: MARSTALLSTR. 8, D-80539 MUNCHEN
DENMARK: DANMUSIK, VOGNMAGERGADE 7 DK 1120 KOBENHAVNK

Acknowledgments:

A warm and loving "thank you" to Deborah Peer, Dan Farr, Colgan Bryan, Aaron Stang, Gwen Dageford, Rebekah West, Bruce Ball, Park Peters, Jeff Shuey, Bob Miller, Andy Svec, Linc Hoke, Linc Luthier, Ralph Heinz, Renkus/Heinz, Kubicki Guitar Technology, GHS Strings, N. S. "Buck" Brundage, A.R.T., Nizar Akhrass, May Audio, Max Cardy III, Peter Coggan, The UCROSS Foundation/Heather Plank, Dr. William Fowler, and my boys Shevek and Sam. I want to thank everyone for their support in the completion of this project.

About the Author:

Dean Peer is an internationally acclaimed solo bass artist and is widely recognized as the authority on the use of bass harmonics. He is also a composer, arranger, and producer with three solo records to date. *Bass Player, Bass Frontiers,* and *Guitar Player* magazines have all published Dean's articles. Dean is the recipient of many awards, including the ASCAP Popular Music Award and a grant from the National Endowment for the Arts. To find out more about his work, visit www.dpartists.com on the Internet.

CONTENTS

FOREWORD

Bass harmonics add texture and nuance to your playing. The purpose of this book is to encourage you to put bass harmonics to practical use by giving you the basics and showing you the possibilities. For reasons of sanity, I assume that you are a knowledgeable musician. Specifically, a chord and chord voicing background will be helpful, and in general, if you feel comfortable with your musical knowledge, you will probably be okay working through this book. Technically speaking, learning harmonics is learning a new technique, so your current technical level is important only to a small degree. What is important is that you want to find out more about bass harmonics.

In terms of how to use this book, the smaller picture is that for every explanation about harmonics there is an accompanying etude to practice and/or a diagram, chart, or photograph to relate to. The bigger picture is that this book goes from simple exercises and ideas to more difficult ones, from the beginning of the book to the end of the book. If you are just starting out with harmonics, work straight through. If you already have some working knowledge of harmonics and you are, for example, interested in finding out about a specific technique, by all means go directly to that point in the book.

The enclosed CD includes examples of bass harmonics and all the musical exercises in this book. While the book and CD are designed to be used in conjunction with one another, you may choose to use the book independently of the recording. Either way works. Have fun with your new challenge.

SYMBOL LEGEND

Harmonic . . . . ○

Stopped note . . . . ●

Harmonic . . . . ◊

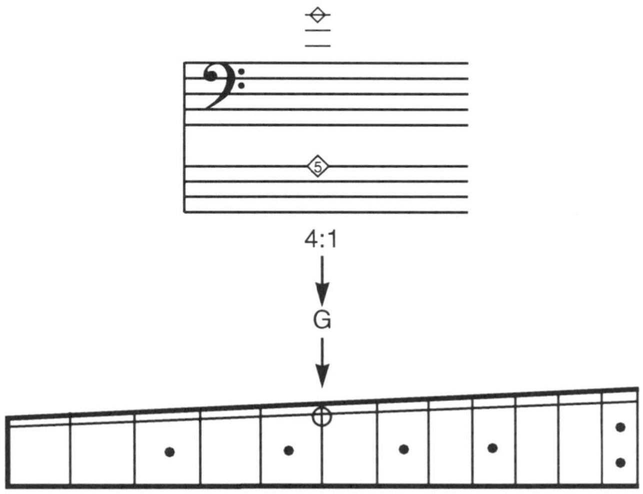

Choice of either stopped note or harmonic . . . .

Optional voice . . . . ⊙

Bent note . . . .

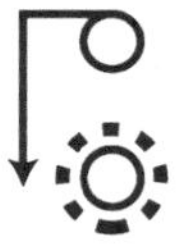

Any note in parentheses has a special explanation near the diagram . . . . (○)

Finger numbering (for etudes) . . . .

Dual node . . . .

PREFACE: THE SCIENCE OF SOUND

PHYSICS

In this preface, I'm going to cover **how harmonics function and how to use them**. We will look at the physics of a vibrating string, **node** and **antinode points** (the points that determine the location of harmonics), how harmonics are labeled, and harmonic ratios. The physics of all vibrating sources do not need to be covered for the sake of looking at bass harmonics. However, you might consider looking at other systems for a deeper understanding.

THE VIBRATING STRING

The vibration of a string is affected by the tension, gauge, and type of string, although it primarily responds according to how it is set into motion. **A string vibrates at many different lengths simultaneously—any of these lengths can be brought out and used as a harmonic.** Figure 1 shows a string vibrating in its most ideal way. Here, you can look at a string as if it were pulled apart and each division demonstrated separately.

Figure 1

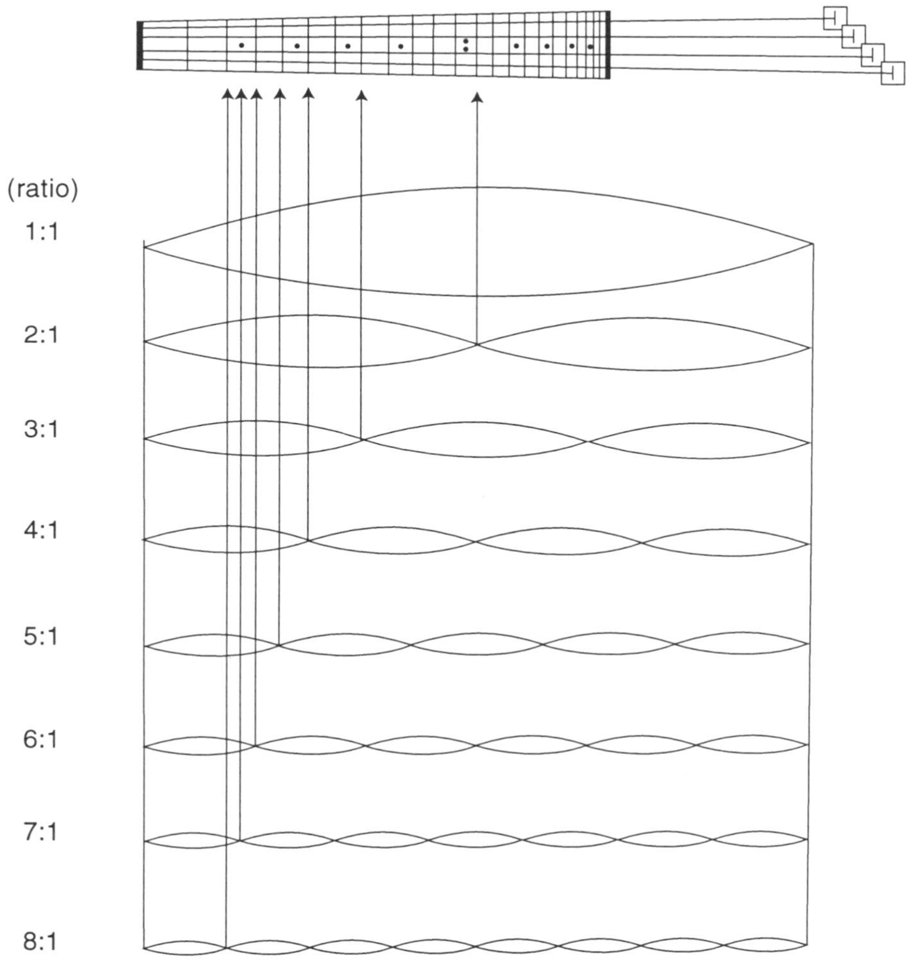

NODE AND ANTINODE POINTS

A node point is a place where there is no sound. It is the pivotal point of a vibrating string. (See Figure 2.) "Antinode" refers to the string at its point of farthest excursion—the point of farthest distance between the vibrations. (See Figure 2.) Generally, harmonics are produced by touching a node point with one finger and plucking one of its antinodes with another finger.

Figure 2

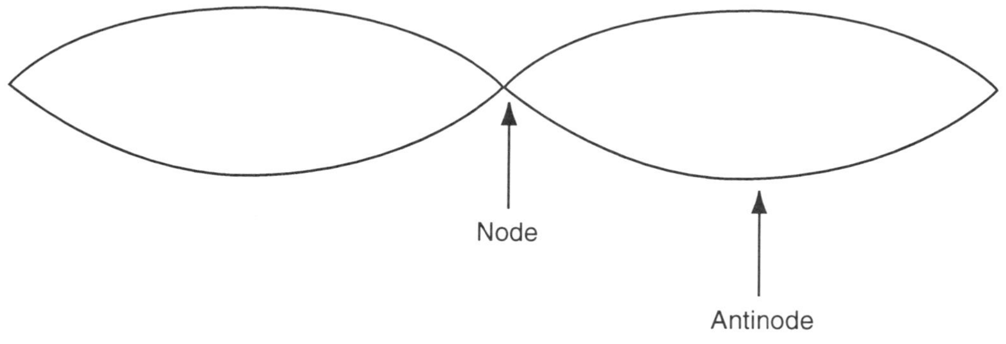

Figure 3

The **fundamental** is the basic pitch of a musical note. When you touch a node point, the fundamental is choked off and the harmonic is allowed to ring. For example, when you pluck a string and at the same time lightly touch it exactly in the middle, you get a harmonic vibrating at twice the rate of the fundamental—or one octave above the freely vibrating string.

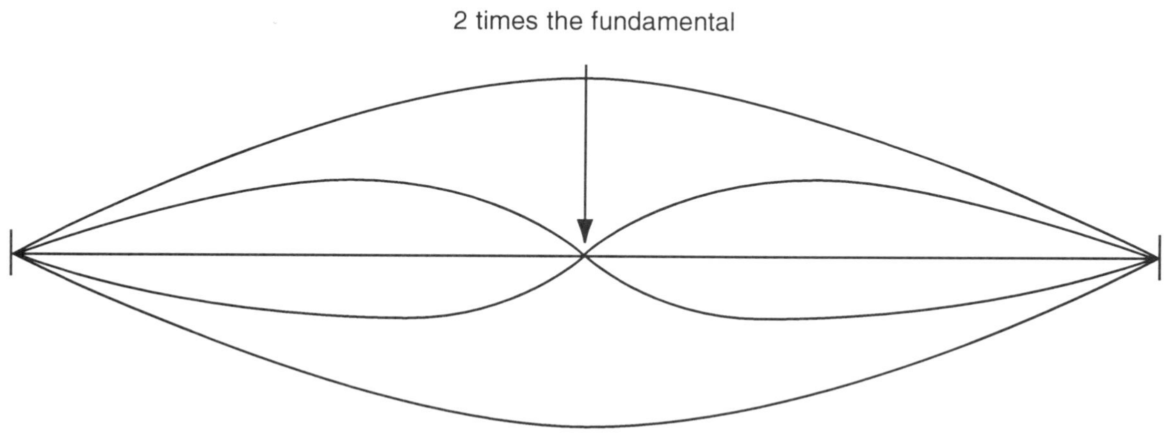

EXPERIMENT TO "SEE" HARMONICS

This experiment is a hands-on look at the harmonic structure of the string without the use of an expensive oscilloscope. It allows you to actually see concepts presented in Figures 1, 2, and 3. For this experiment, you need the following:

1) A television tuned in to a blank channel (or any other light source that can flash about 30 times per second).

2) A rubber band or a piece of elastic cord (acting as a string under tension).

3) A dark room (not necessary, but helpful).

With both hands, hold the rubber band or elastic cord vertically in front of the TV set. Pull, stretch, and pluck the experimental string in as many ways as you can think of (i.e., tie it in knots or try it under different tensions.) (See Figure 4.)

Figure 4

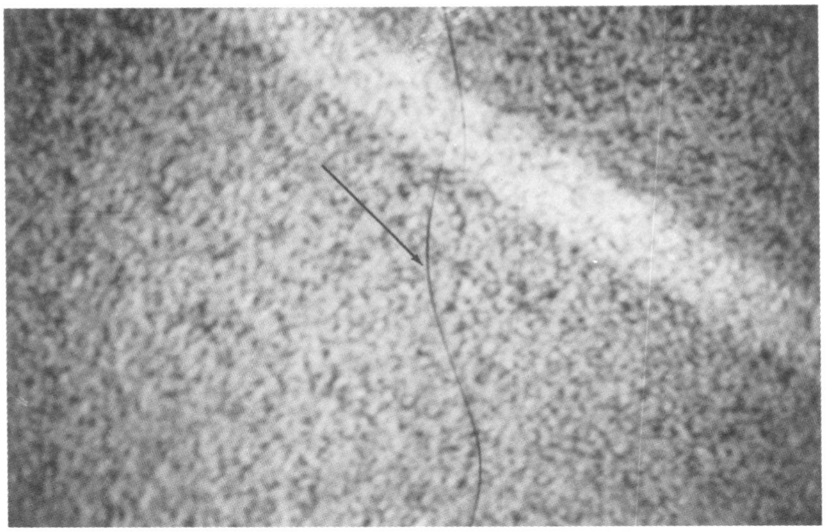

1) Observe the type of waveform. It is possible to find the four waveforms shown in Figure 5 if you experiment by plucking at different points, lengths, and tensions.

2) Observe the waveforms as they dissipate.

Figure 5

You can also situate your bass so that you line up either the E or G string, the TV, and your eye to where you can see the actual waveforms coming off of your bass string as you pluck it.

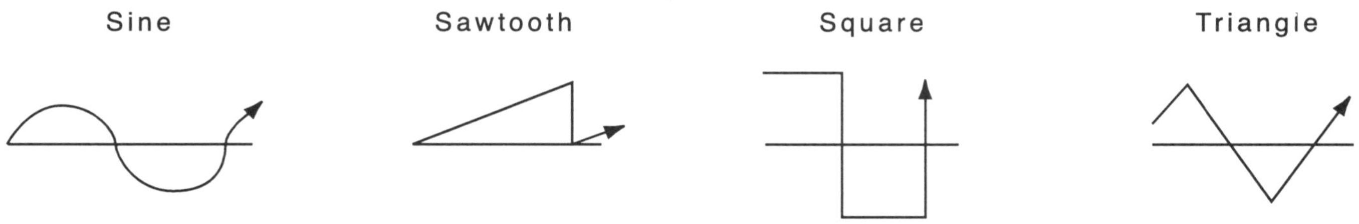

LABELING FREQUENCY COMPONENTS

Humans seem to have a need to label, and, for as many humans as there are, we have as many labels—which brings us to Figure 6.

Harmonics can be labeled as follows. These labels are universal, and this table will help you keep it all straight. For the purpose of simplicity, in this book we will use the term "ratio" to label a harmonic's relationship to its fundamental.

Figure 6

SYSTEM OF NAMING FREQUENCY COMPONENTS

Ratios	=	Harmonics	=	Overtones	=	Partials
1:1		Fundamental		Fundamental		1st partial
2:1		2nd harmonic		1st overtone		2nd partial
3:1		3rd harmonic		2nd overtone		3rd partial
4:1		4th harmonic		3rd overtone		4th partial

HARMONICS EXPRESSED AS RATIOS

Figure 7 lays out the tempered scale, the ratio, the chord tone, the letter name, the distance from the fundamental, and their relationships for each harmonic on the G string. These relationships work for any string regardless of its tuning. You can visualize where the overtone series and the tempered scale overlap.

Figure 7

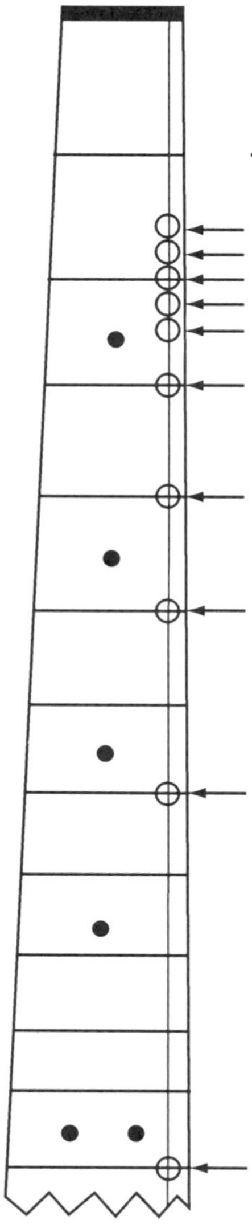

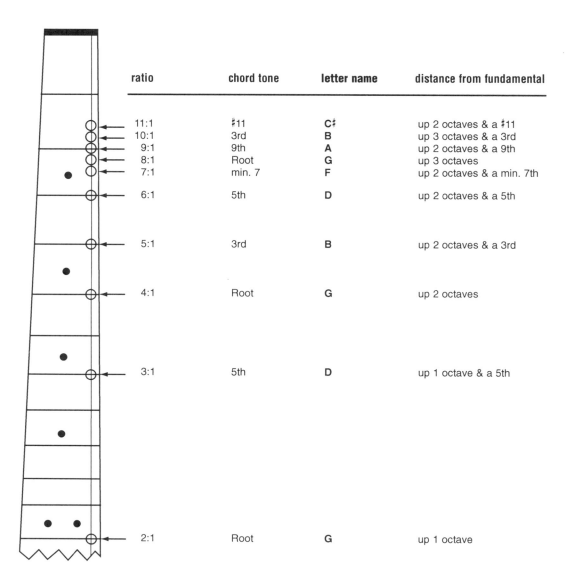

ratio	chord tone	letter name	distance from fundamental
11:1	♯11	**C♯**	up 2 octaves & a ♯11
10:1	3rd	**B**	up 3 octaves & a 3rd
9:1	9th	**A**	up 2 octaves & a 9th
8:1	Root	**G**	up 3 octaves
7:1	min. 7	**F**	up 2 octaves & a min. 7th
6:1	5th	**D**	up 2 octaves & a 5th
5:1	3rd	**B**	up 2 octaves & a 3rd
4:1	Root	**G**	up 2 octaves
3:1	5th	**D**	up 1 octave & a 5th
2:1	Root	**G**	up 1 octave

Figure 8

You may notice that the distance between harmonics is reduced as you move away from the 12th fret, toward the bridge and toward the nut. Starting at the 12th fret and going in either direction, you also see that an exact mirror of the overtone series exists.

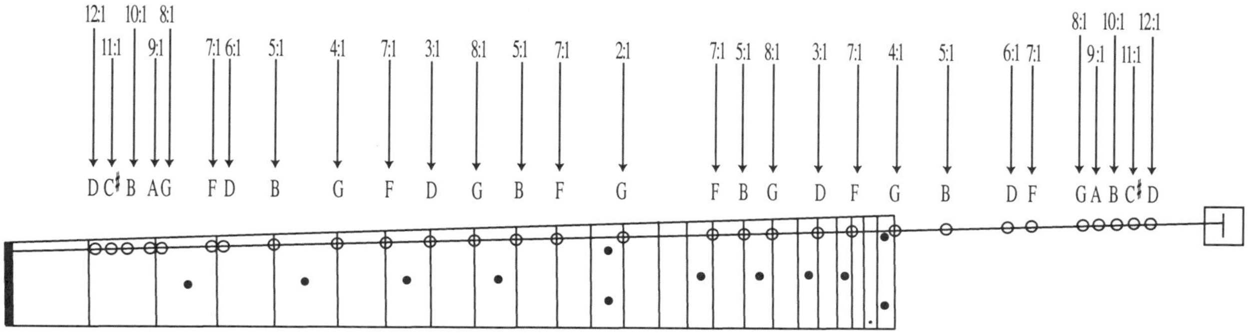

Figure 9

In Figure 9, harmonic ratios are listed for the G string. Harmonic ratios from 2:1 to 8:1 are considered primary because it is easy to get them to "speak" (make a clear sound). The secondary ratios, from 9:1 to 12:1, do not "speak" as easily and the capacity to use them is more limited.

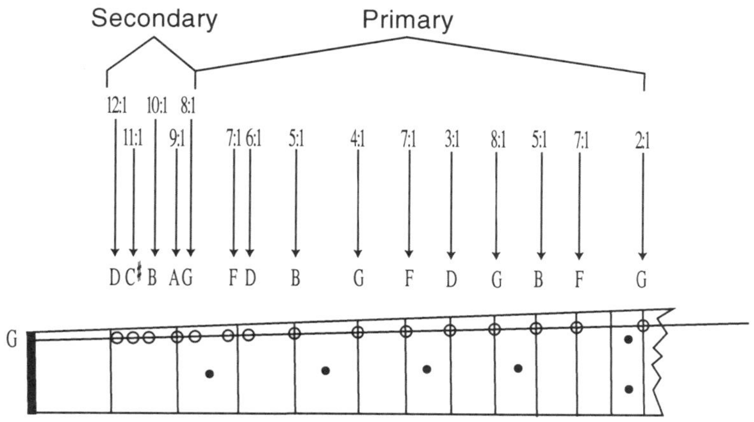

Figure 10 depicts for each string the available harmonics, their harmonic ratio, actual pitch, and where they lie on the fingerboard.

Figure 10

E String

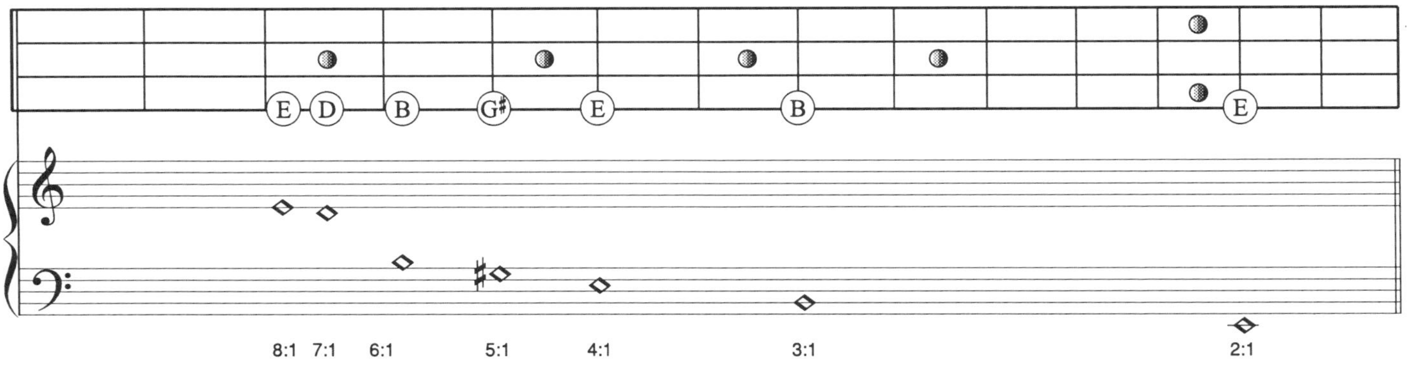

A String

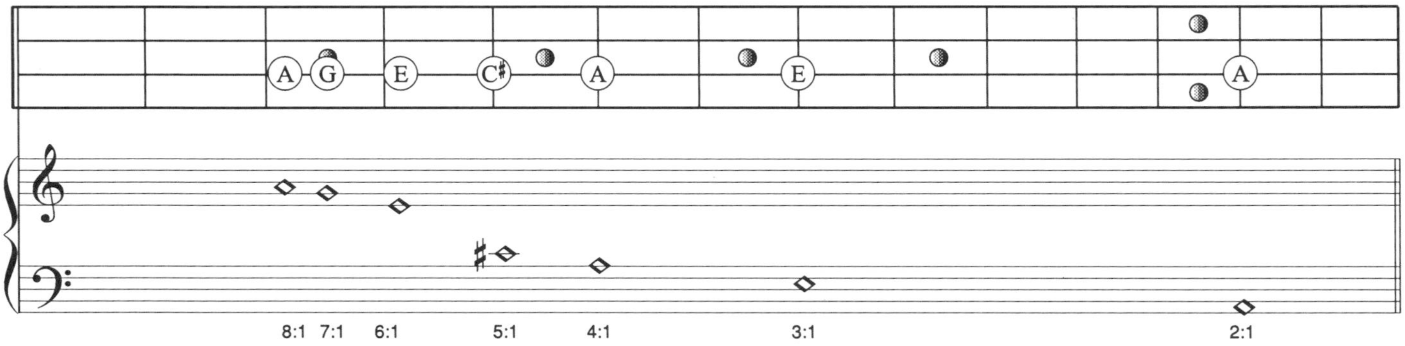

D String

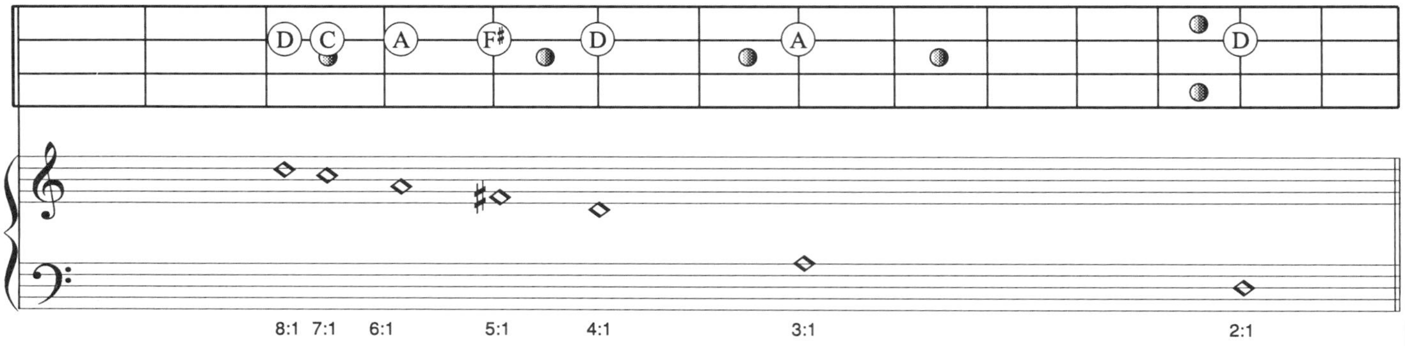

G String

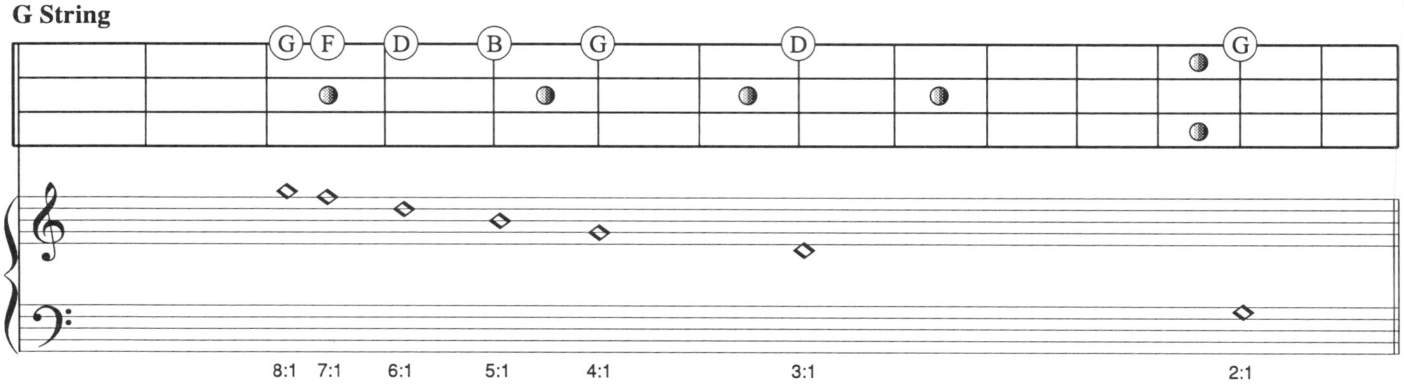

CHAPTER 1: BUILDING BLOCKS

Several options become available to the bassist who uses the expanded range of harmonics. Instead of being limited to the traditional warm, fat sound of the bass, you also have access to the thin, bell-like sound of the higher register unique to harmonics. The following systematic method shows which notes are available as harmonics and where they are.

WHERE HARMONICS ARE

To begin assembling a method of locating harmonic notes, I'd like to offer several points of information. These points contain the fundamental ingredients needed to systematically unravel the relationship between the fretted scale on the neck and the overtone series that exists on each string.

A single vibrating string's natural set of usable harmonics provides a dominant 7 (♯11) chord. Knowing this, you can easily name the possible harmonics for any given string. No matter what tuning you set up, the harmonics will always be in the same place in relation to the fingerboard. (See Figure 11.)

Figure 11

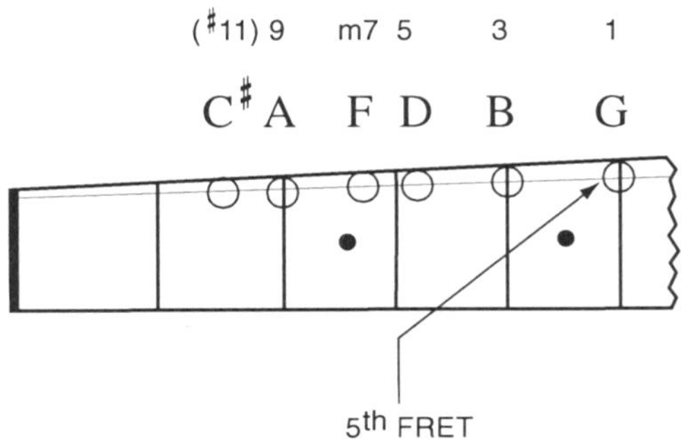

To begin to name the notes quickly and to minimize confusion, refer to Figure 12. It shows the breakdown of harmonics into three groups: Group 1 outlines a simple triad; Group 2 outlines a dom. 7 chord; and Group 3 is a succession of whole steps. Groups 2 and 3 combined provide a dom. 7 (♯11) chord. Now to find your way around, you need to know the name of the string and basic chord spelling. To build a chord, you begin at the 12th and 5th frets with the letter name of the string. (See Figure 12.)

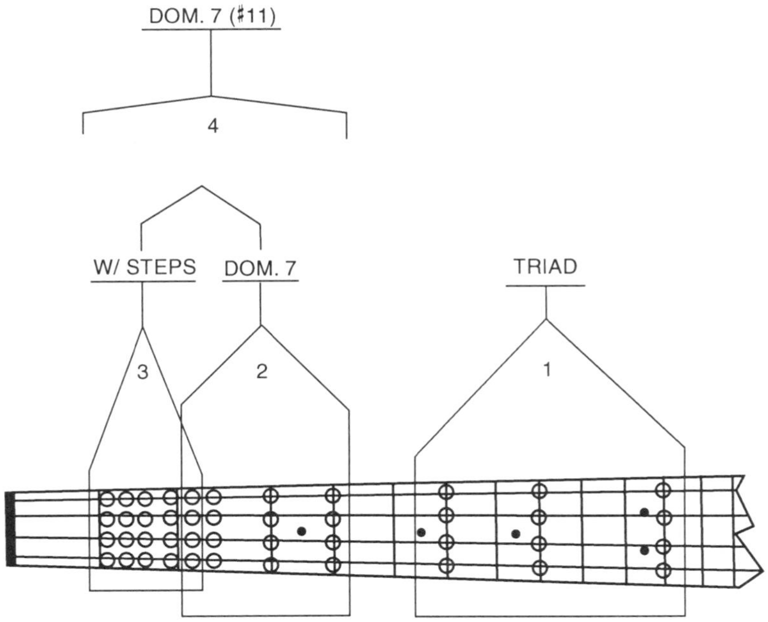

Figure 12
The upper strata of notes in Group 3 (from the 8:1 ratio up) are increasingly difficult to use because the node points are smaller and the speaking length of the string is shorter than those in the middle of the string. Group 2 provides the single-hand position where you can reach every available harmonic without any shifting.

As you explore the range and location of harmonics, you will find that many are not quite in tune with the scale on the neck. This is mainly true of harmonics of odd-numbered ratios. Having to contend with intonation differences is something to be dealt with case by case (i.e., masking by electronic means like flanging and chorusing, or living with it).

CHAPTER 2: BASIC TECHNIQUE

We have looked at how the building blocks of the harmonic system work in theoretical terms. We need now to turn our attention to the physical aspect—the technique. To play harmonics, it is necessary to look at what the right and left hands are doing individually and together. We will also cover using stopped bass notes.

Keep in mind as you are working through this chapter that individual harmonics respond differently to the same touch in terms of volume and tonal quality. You will learn to balance these differences.

RIGHT HAND

Observe in the photograph of the right hand that the wrist is in a flat position in order to allow complete freedom of movement. Since you will cover more strings for more purposes, your hand will be in a different position than usual. (See Figure 13.)

Figure 13

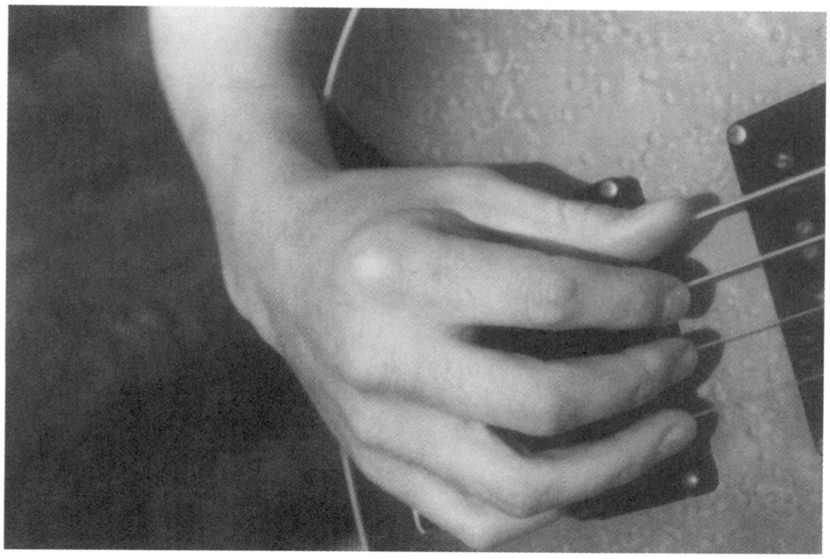

Figure 14

Where you pluck has a great deal to do with how clear and at what volume a harmonic sounds. This is particularly evident as you go higher in ratio where harmonics are crowded together. The optimum place to pluck a harmonic is at its antinode, and making use of antinodes is vital. However, the way to approach finding the best place to pluck is by feel alone. "Earball" it. Figure 14 shows the node and antinode points in a 4:1 ratio.

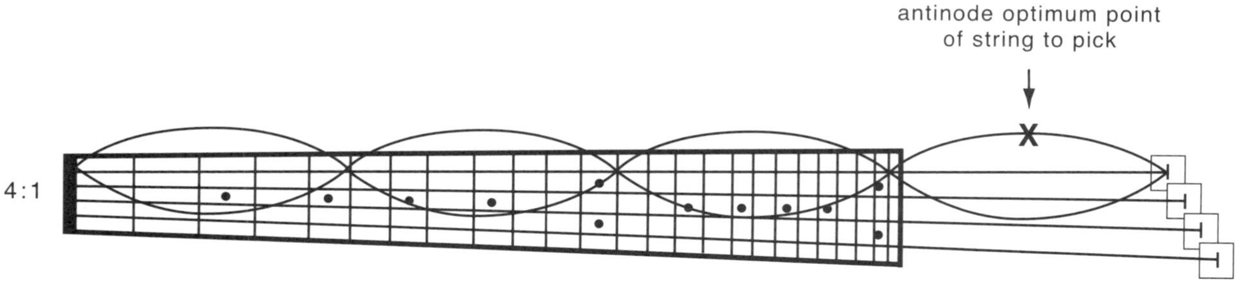

Figure 15

CD TRACK 2

The right hand's function is altered from what could be called standardized electric bass technique because instead of plucking with just two fingers (first and second), you add your thumb and third finger. The following etude provides practice for this right-hand action.

Using four fingers rather than two allows you to play each string individually (single notes) or simultaneously (chords).

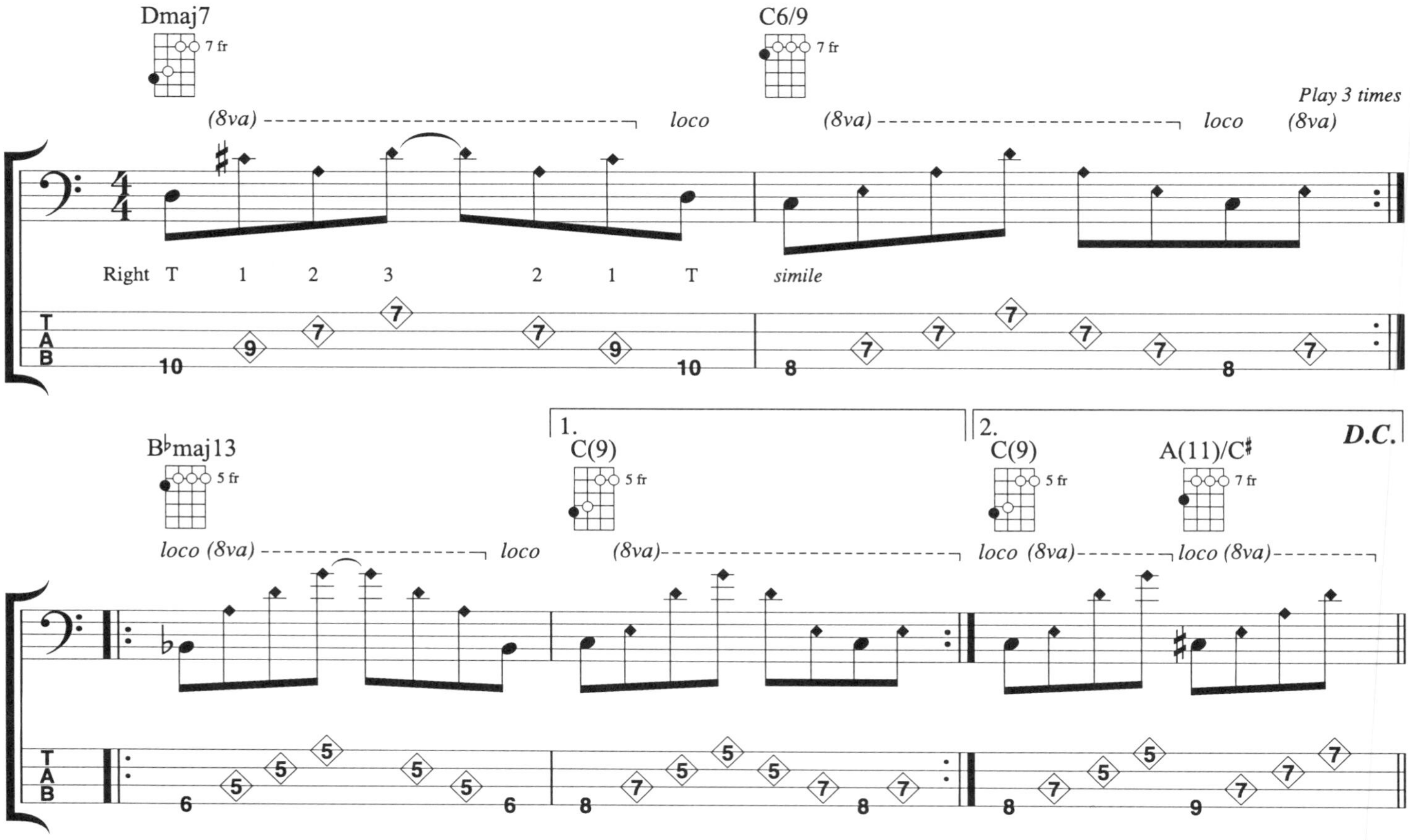

LEFT HAND

To play harmonics, put your left hand in a position that employs economy of movement. Relax your hand and slightly curl your fingers to maximize leverage for stopped notes and control for harmonics. The left hand has the role of creating two different sounds, either separately or together, when touching the string. Figure 16 demonstrates how to blend the sounds of both stopped notes and harmonics within a single chord.

Figure 16

CD TRACK 3

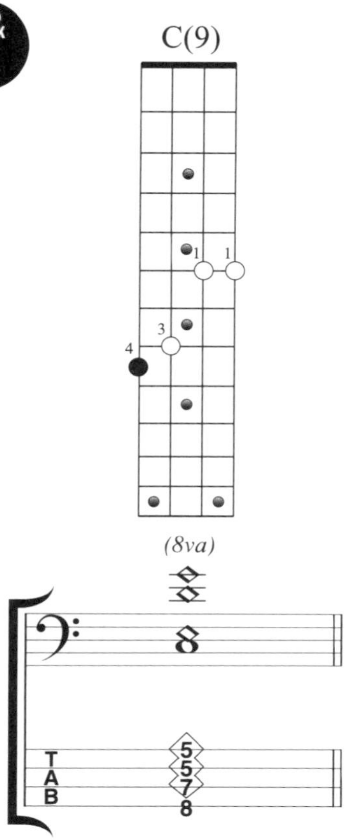

At first, playing stopped notes and harmonics are separate sensations, but you begin to fuse the two into one solid sensation as you become accustomed to the feel. In the beginning your touch will seem light and uncertain, but soon with practice you will grab harmonic chords and scales decisively. Your fingers become familiar with a new margin for error, and the harmonics begin to feel as solid as the stopped notes. It is as though the node points become notches for your fingers. What happens is that your subconscious begins to record the necessary parameters for chord forms and scales, and you learn the margin for error.

APPLYING STOPPED BASS NOTES

Consider using this technique:

1) simply play block, or arpeggiated, chords consisting of both stopped and harmonic notes, and/or
2) use the stopped bass notes and harmonic notes separately (i.e., for bass line and melody). (See Figure 17.)

Figure 17

CD TRACK 4

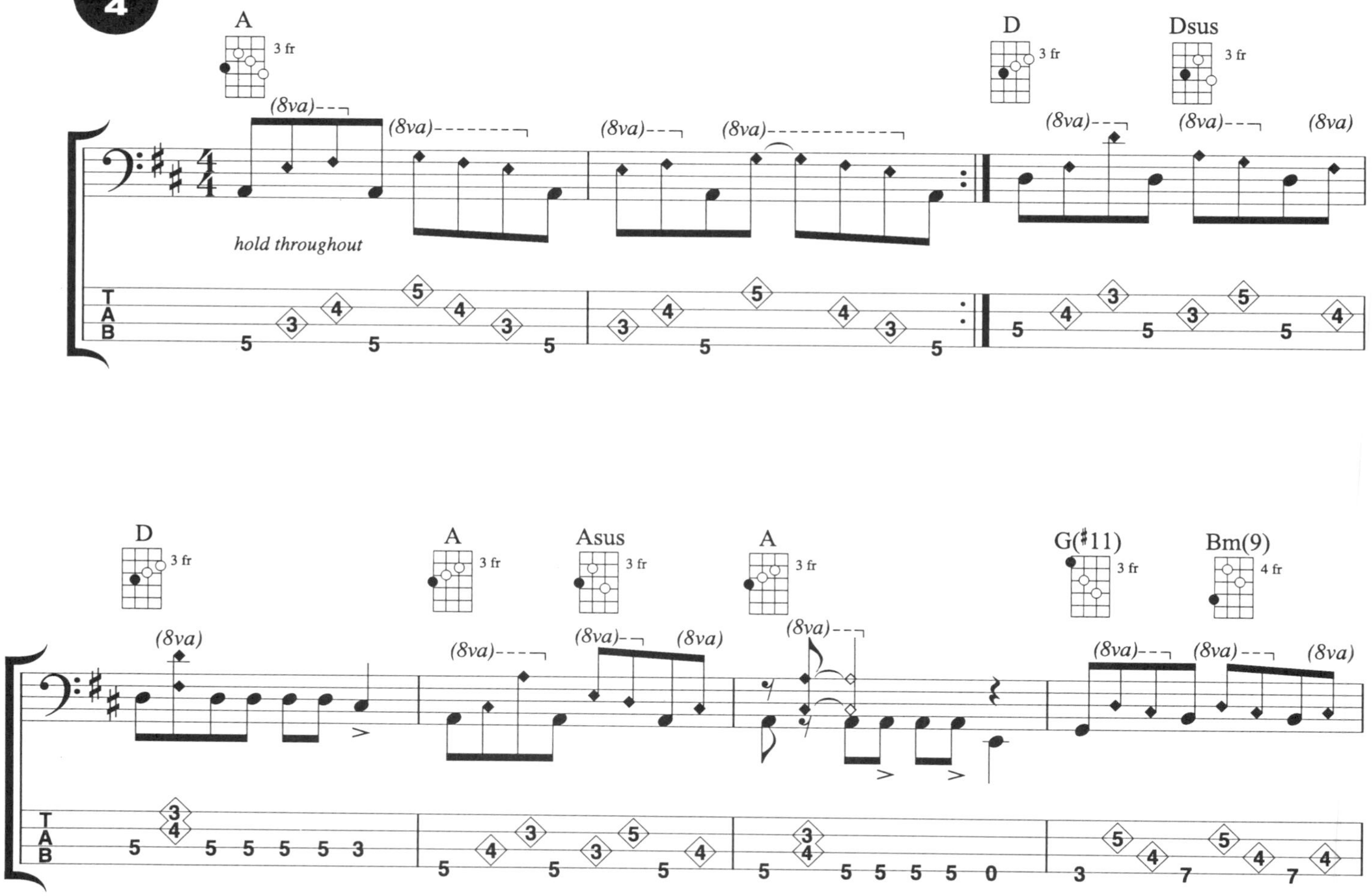

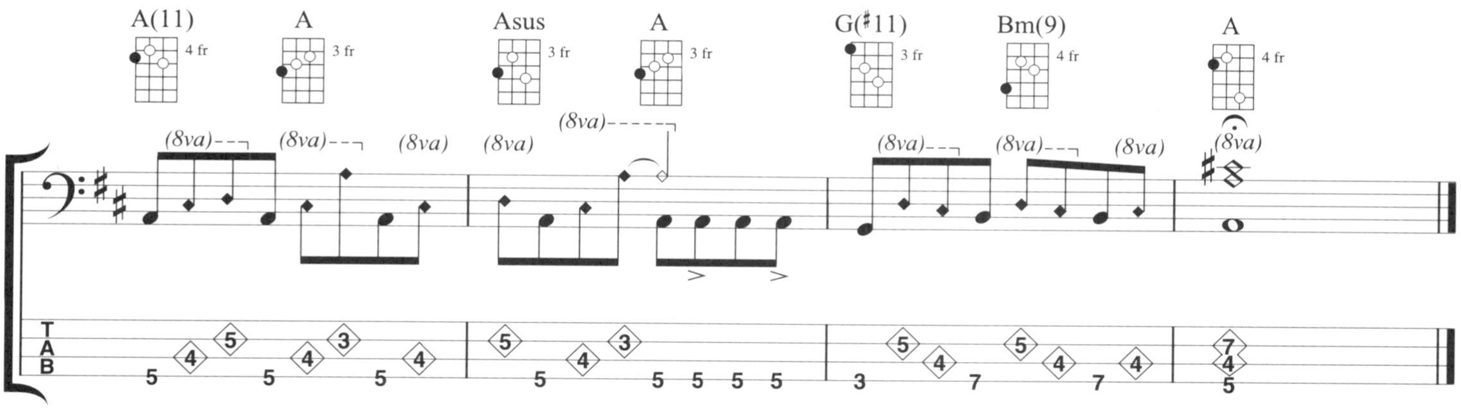

When using stopped bass notes as chord tones, the lower you go down the neck, the wider you must keep the intervals between stopped notes. This keeps them from becoming muddled, and is true mainly of the bottom register on the E string from about A natural on down. (Because of differences in the string gauges and corresponding sounds of stopped and harmonic notes, it is generally convenient to play your stopped bass notes on the E and A strings. However, you *can* play stopped bass notes and harmonic notes on any of the strings.)

CHAPTER 3: SCALES AND CHORDS

Now that your hands are acquainted with the functions of playing harmonics and blending harmonics with stopped notes, you are ready to apply basic musical concepts.

SCALES

The bass is already a working "scalar" instrument, but when using harmonics to play scales it is not as straightforward. The **diatonic** D major scale is the single available Ionian scale in standard tuning. The scale tones set the stage for a **diatonic** rather than a chromatic one. The rest of the available scales are E Dorian, F♯ Phrygian, G Lydian, A Mixolydian, B Aeolian, and C♯ Locrian.

Now, let's look at the harmonics available in standard tuning and see what notes can be used for scale or chord tones. Figure 18 shows the bass in standard tuning, the letter names of the actual harmonics available, and a chromatic list of notes. Notice in this list and on the bass neck that B♭ and E♭ are not available.

Figure 18

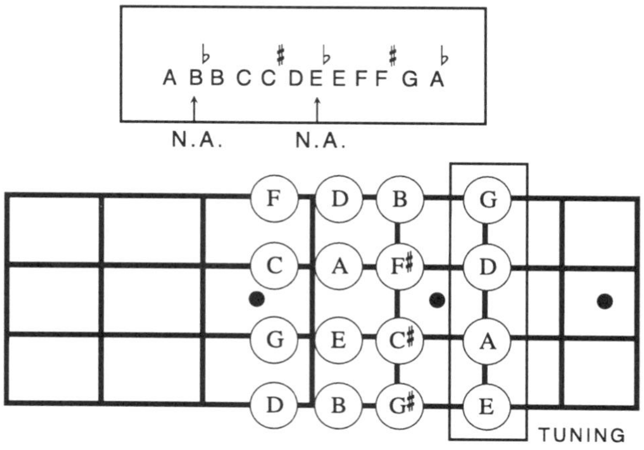

Figure 19

CD TRACK 5

Figure 19 lays out the movement of scale tones 1 through 8. Take note of the zigzag pattern as a visual aid. Also notice the use of the dual node points (D.N.) to enhance the clarity of the 7th scale degree. (See Chapter 5: Dual Node Harmonics, page 36, for an explanation of dual nodes.)

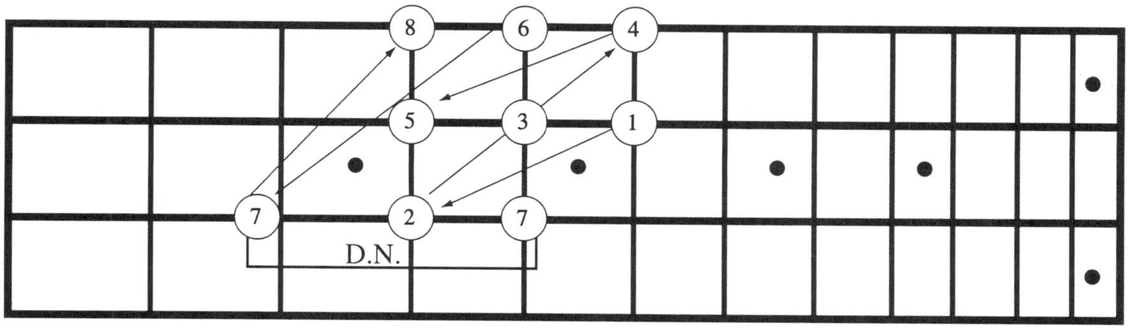

Many other notes are in different octaves which prevent playing a continuous progression of 1/2 steps, although you can get some of these through the use of special techniques presented later.

Stopped bass notes essentially fill in holes in the chromatic scale in order to become, at least, "semi-chromatic." This allows you to play in keys other than D major, and you break up the diatonic constraints a little bit.

CHORDS

Using harmonics to build chords is unique in both sound and application. To be able to convey the basic idea of a chord or tonal center, you are often faced with limitations and choices. We will look at chord position and voicing as a basis of understanding what can be accomplished.

Instead of memorizing all of the patterns, it is necessary to know how to assemble chords. In general, this method of assembly involves knowing the name and position of all the harmonics and finding enough chord voices to establish a chord's color or tonal center.

Included here is a select list of chords for reference to get you started on the right track. (See Figure 20: Select List of Chords.)

Figure 20: Select List of Chords

While using the select list of chords, apply the following rules of thumb:

1) Flat keys are the hardest to play—the more flats, the more difficult because you have fewer necessary harmonic notes available.
2) There is sometimes more than one stopped bass note applied.
3) There is sometimes more than one node point applied to a single string. (Dual node.)
4) In many cases, even in combining stopped bass notes and harmonics, there are just enough voices to establish the chord or tonal center.

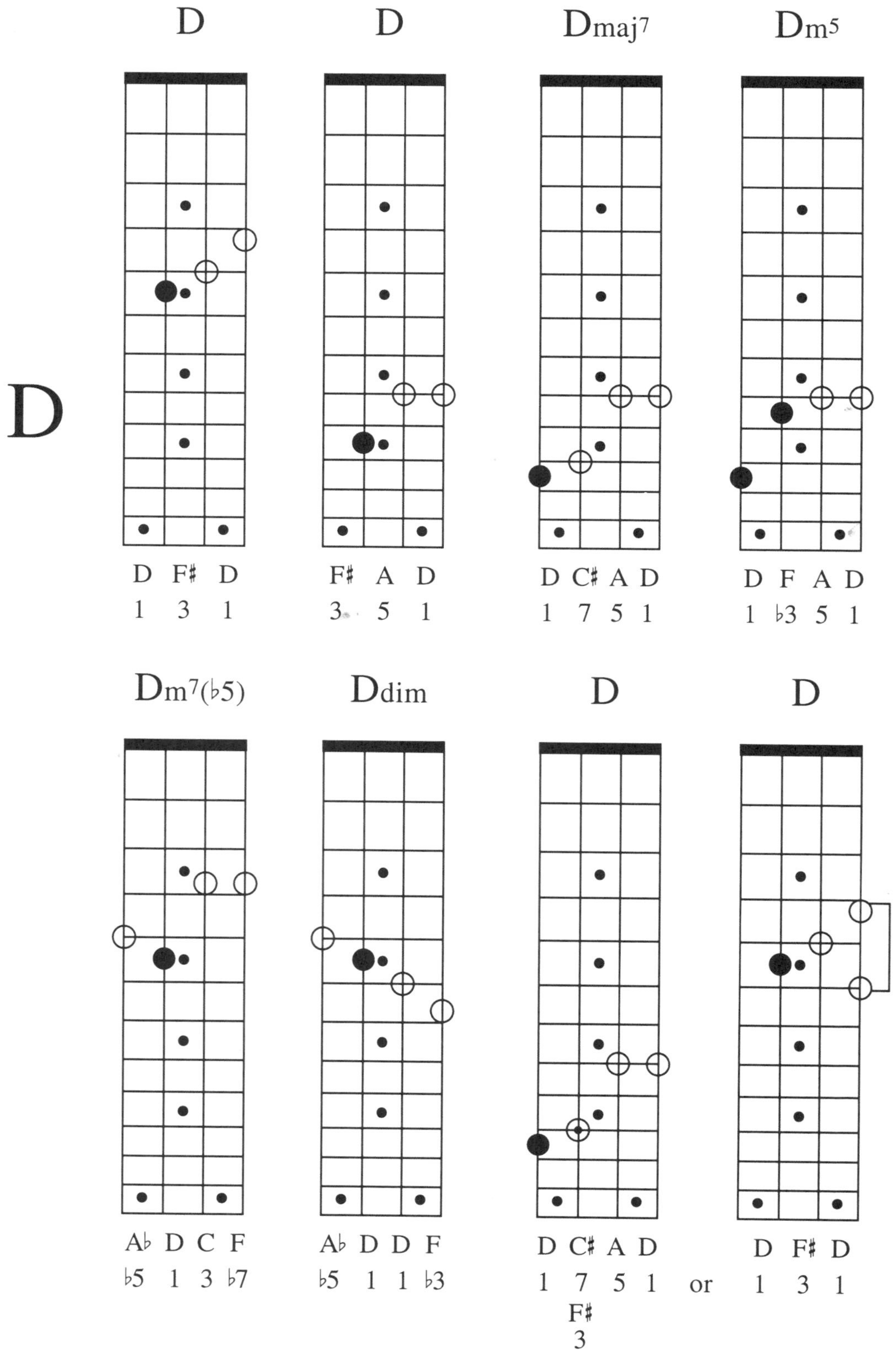

G

G

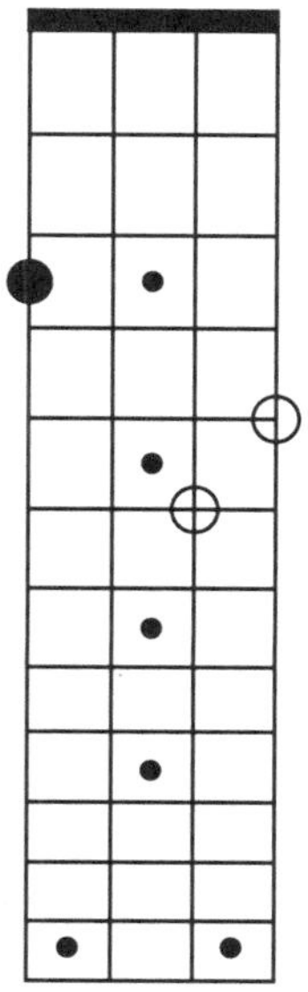

G D B
1 5 3

Gmaj7

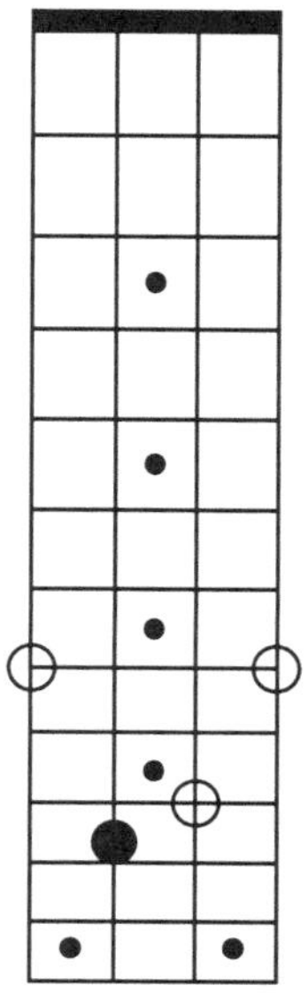

B G F♯ D
3 1 7 5

Gm5

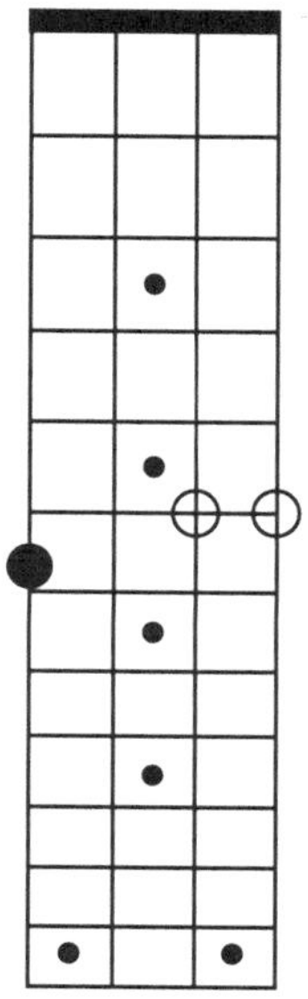

B♭ D G
♭3 5 1

C

Cmaj7

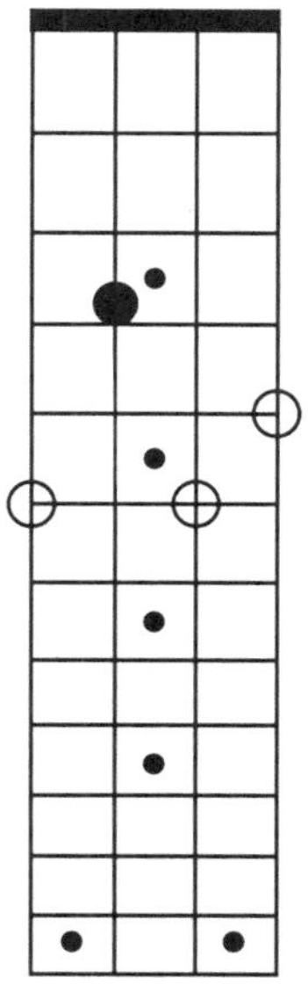

E C D B
3 1 9 7

C(♯11)

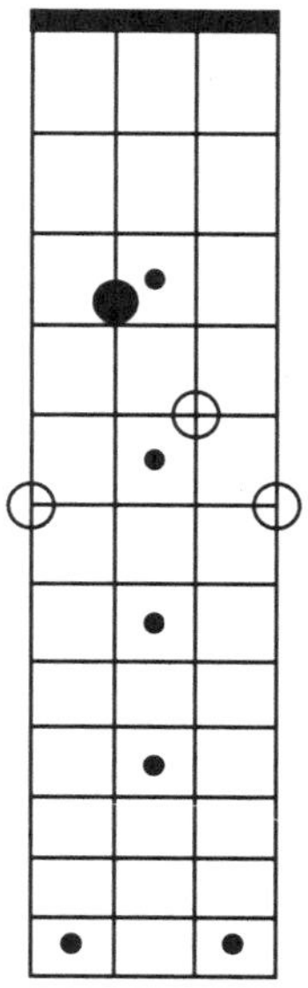

E C F♯ G
3 1 ♯11 5

C(9)

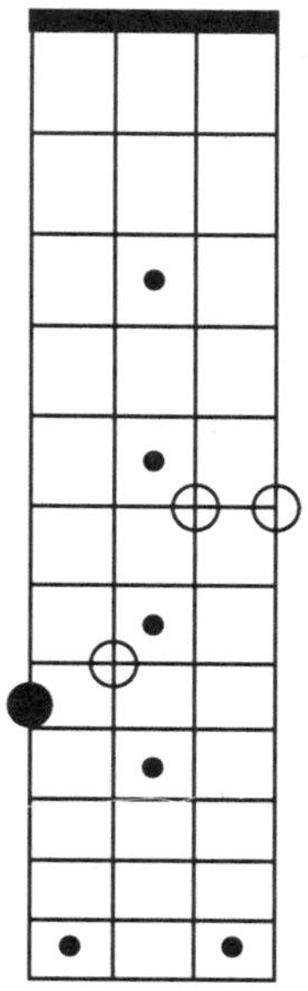

D E D G
1 3 9 5

Cm(9)

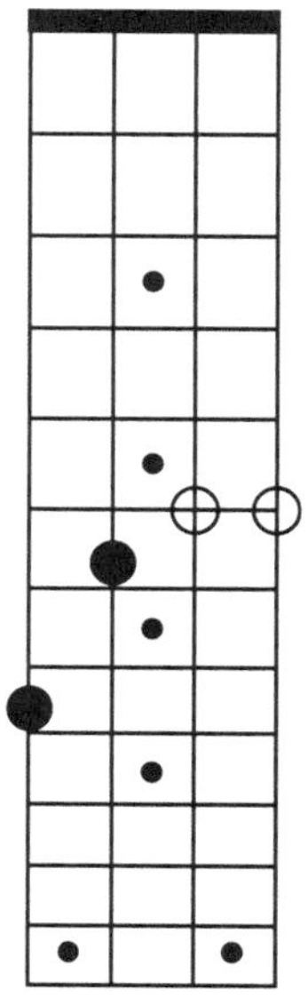

C E♭ D G
1 ♭3 9 5

Cdim

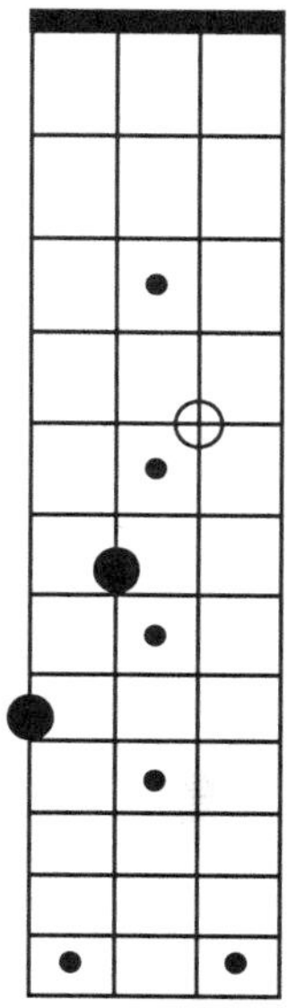

C E♭ G♭
1 ♭3 ♭5

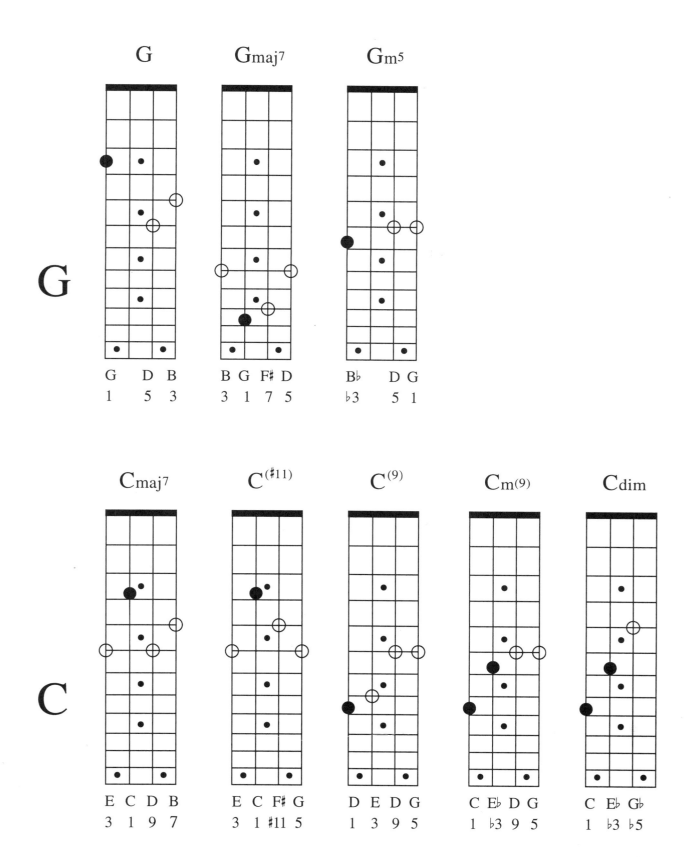

F

Fmaj7

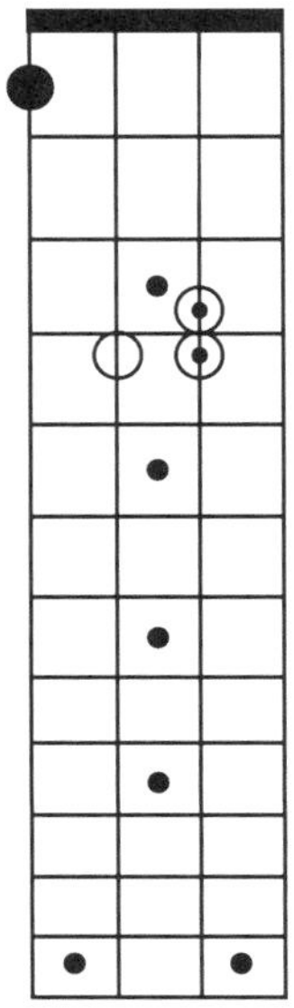

F E A or C
1 7 3 or 5

Faug

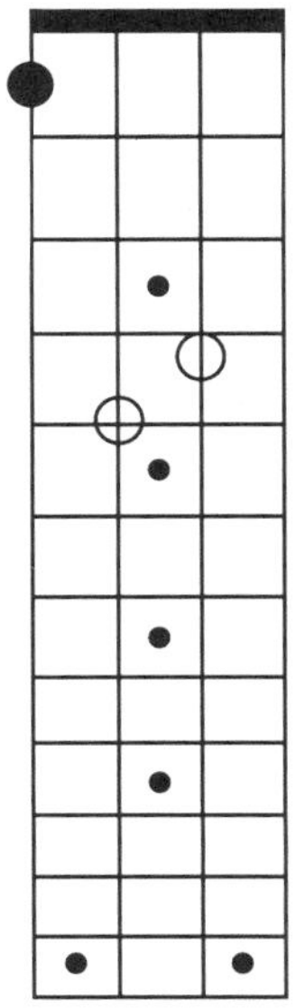

F C♯ A
1 ♯5 3

F(9)

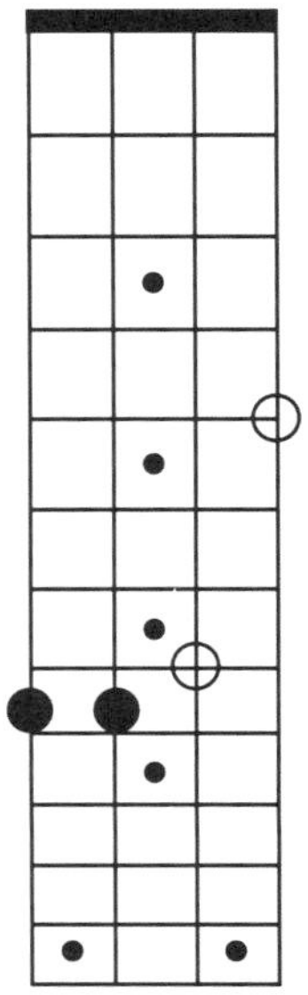

C F A G
5 1 3 9

Fdim

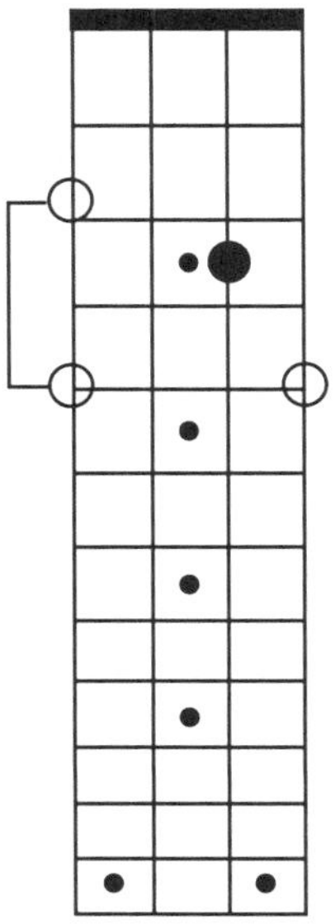

A♭ F C♭
♭3 1 ♭5

B♭

B♭maj13

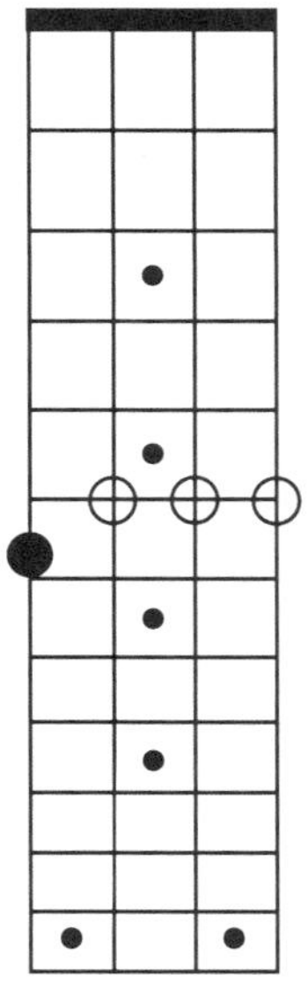

B♭ A D G
1 7 3 6

B♭m

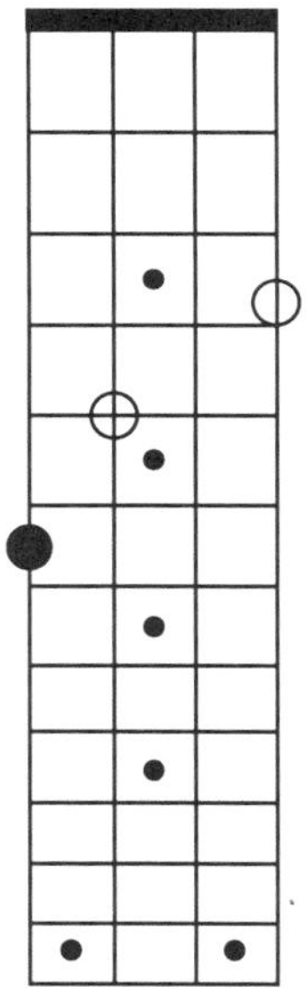

B♭ D♭ F
1 ♭3 5

B♭dim7

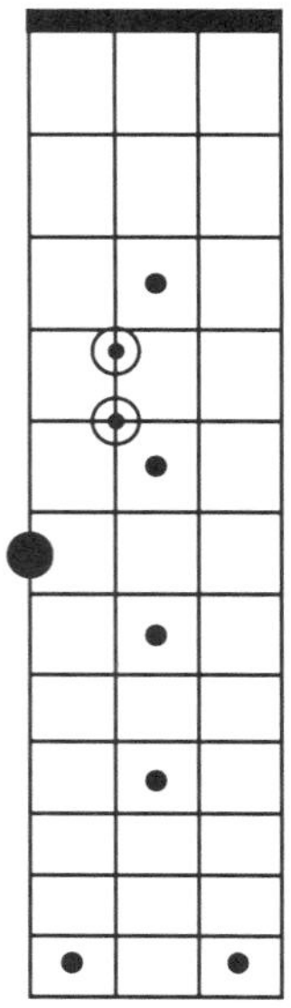

B♭ D♭
1 ♭3
or
F♭
♭5

E♭

E♭maj^7

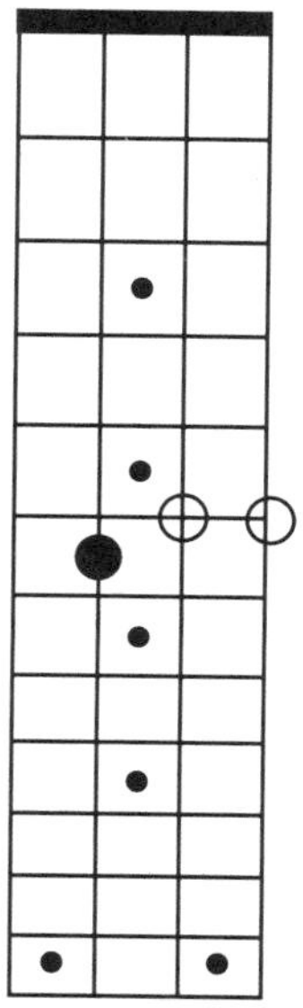

E♭ D G
1 7 3

E$^{♭7}$

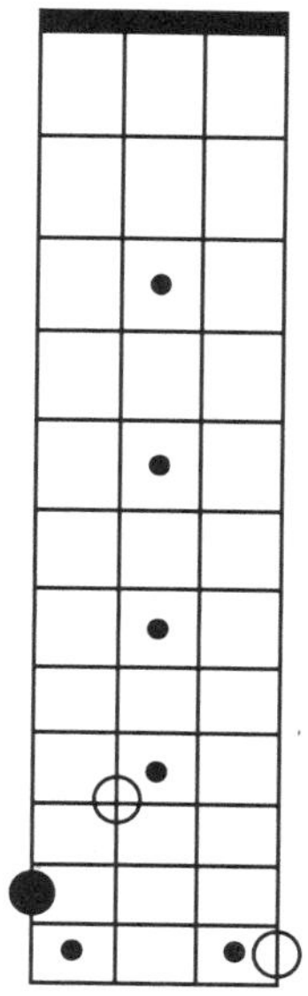

E♭ D♭ G
1 ♭7 3

E$^♭$m

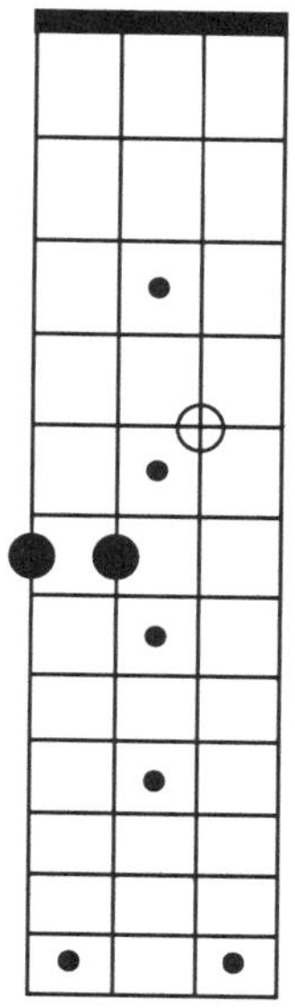

B♭ E♭ G♭
5 1 ♭3

E$^♭$m^7

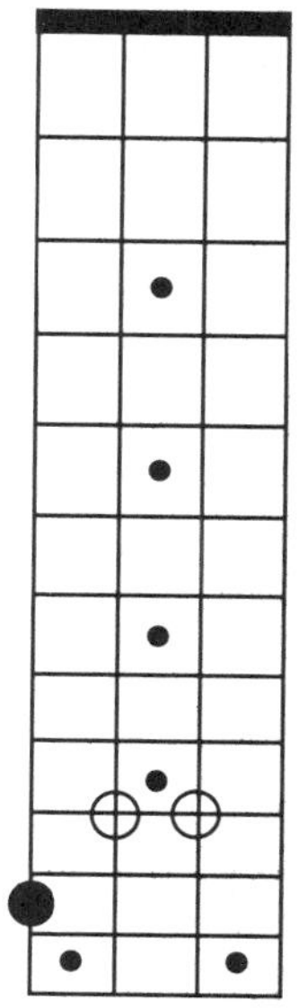

E♭ D♭ G♭
1 ♭7 ♭3

A

A$^♭$

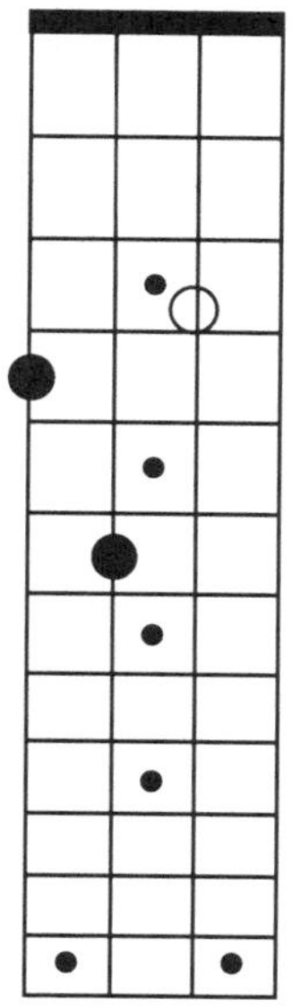

A♭ E♭ C
1 5 3

A$^♭$m

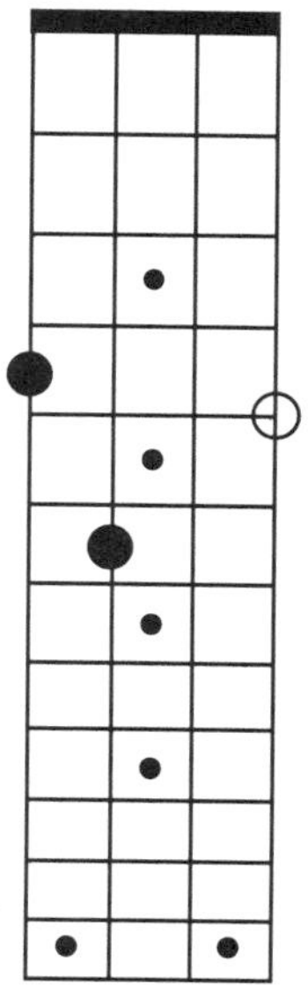

A♭ E♭ C♭
1 5 ♭3

A$^♭$m^7

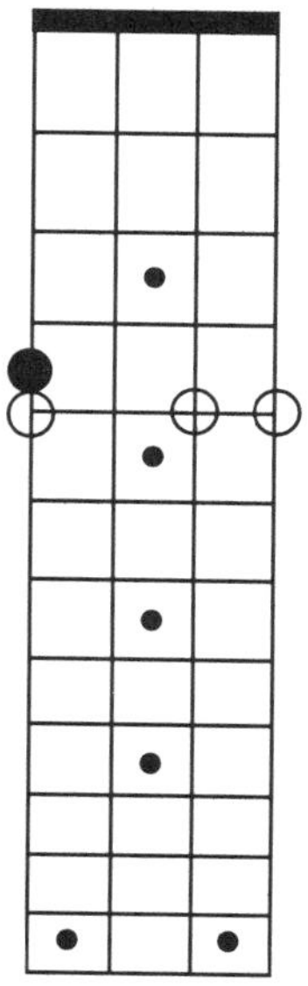

A♭ G♭ C♭
1 ♭7 ♭3

A$^♭$m^7(♭5)

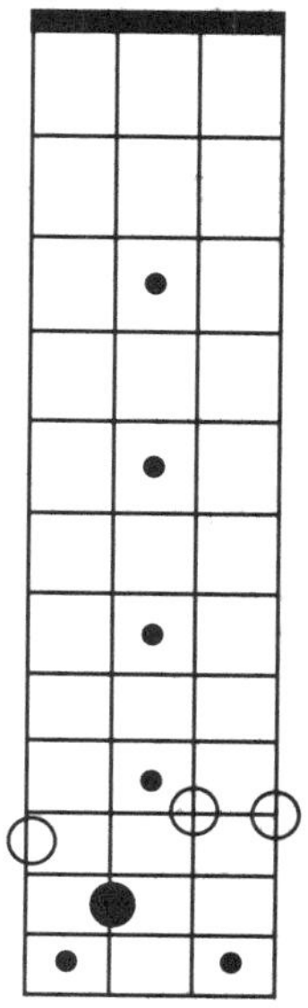

E♭♭ A♭ G♭ C♭
♭5 1 ♭7 ♭3

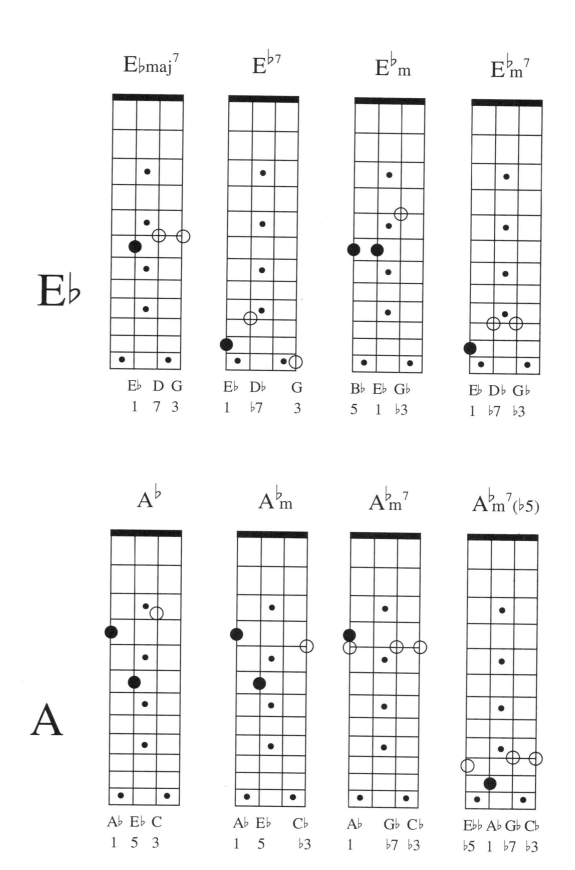

D♭

D♭dim

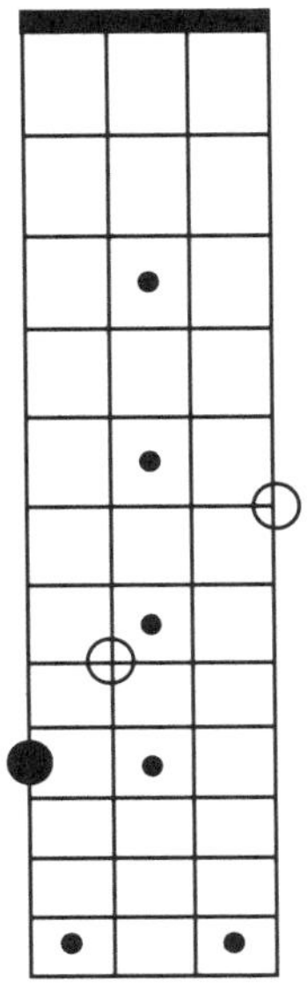

D♭ F♭ A♭♭
1 ♭3 ♭5

D♭m

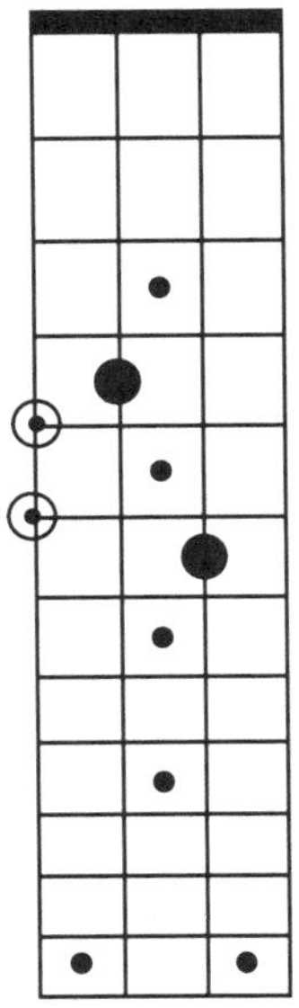

F♭ D♭ A♭
♭3 1 5
or
A♭
5

F♯

F♯

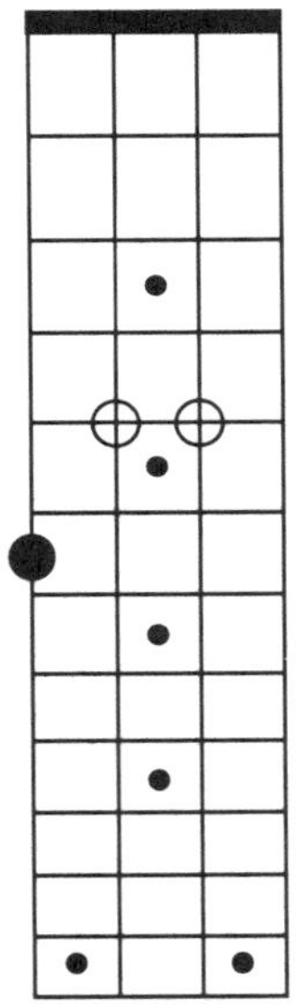

A♯ C♯ F♯
3 5 1

F♯m

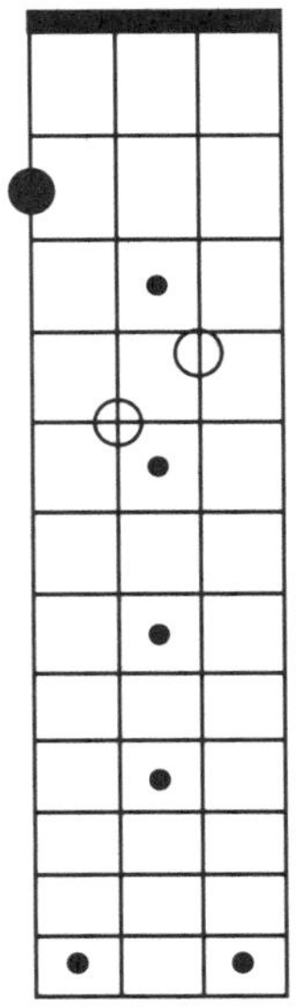

F♯ C♯ A
1 5 ♭3

F♯m7

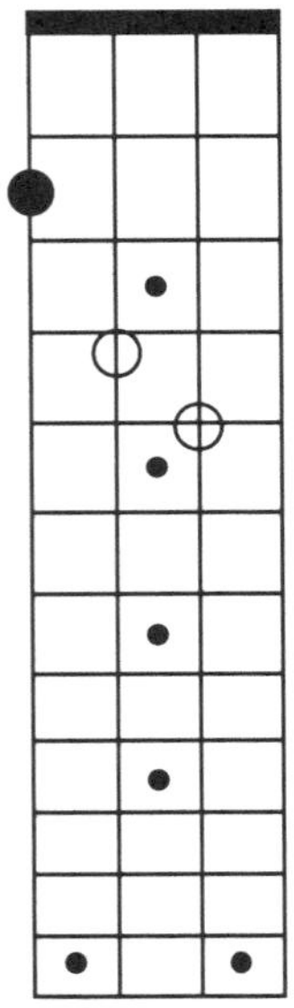

F♯ E F♯
1 ♭7 8

F♯dim

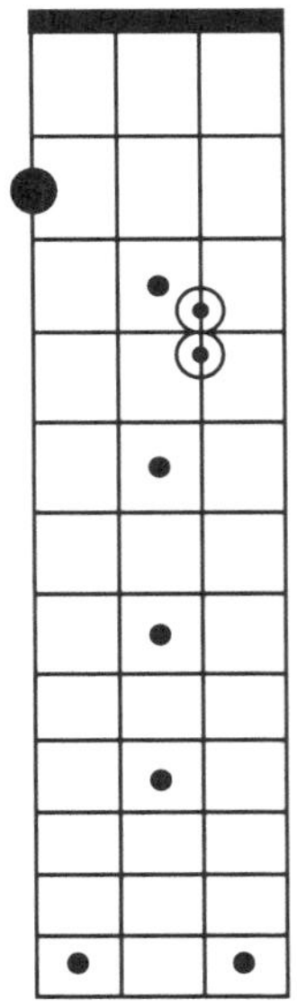

F♯ A
1 ♭3
or
C
♭5

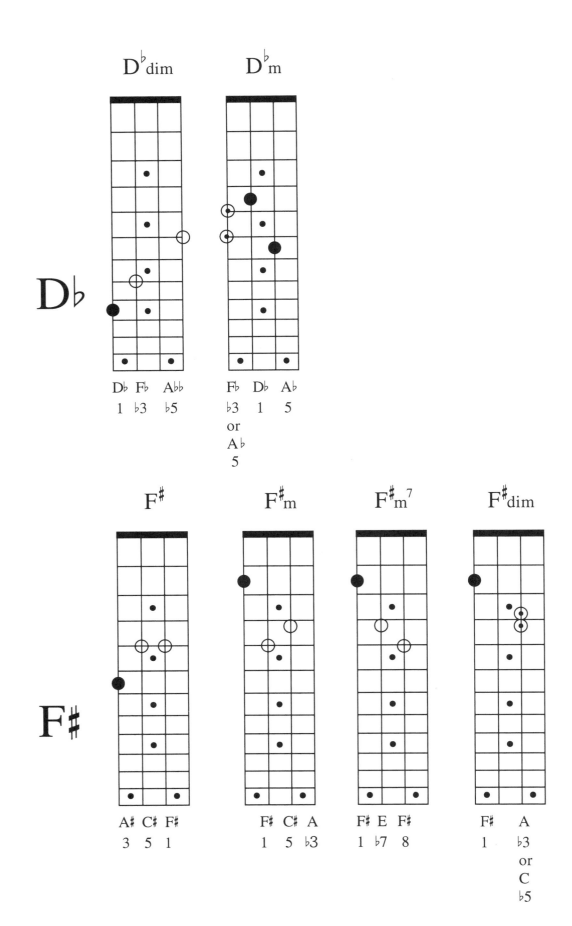

B

B

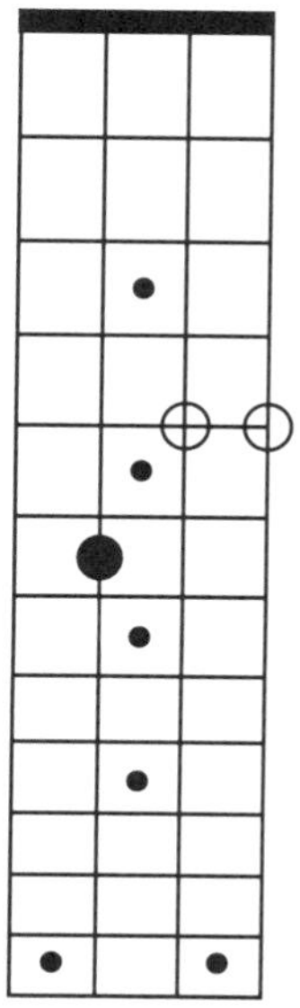

Bm

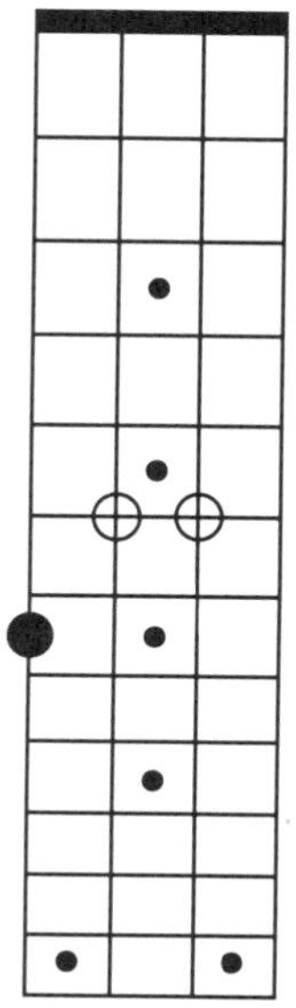

Bm7(♭5)

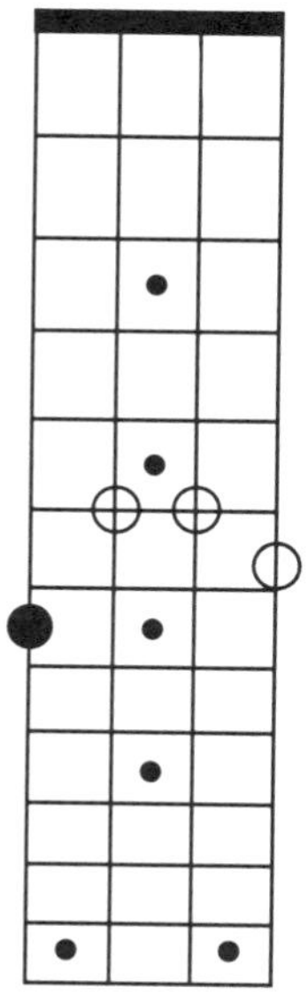

Bdim

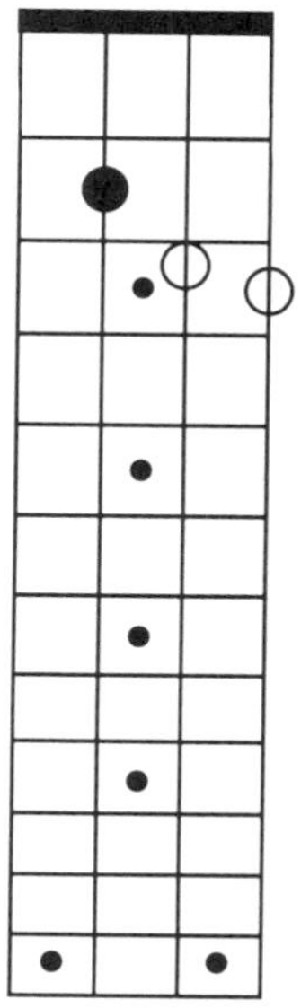

E

E

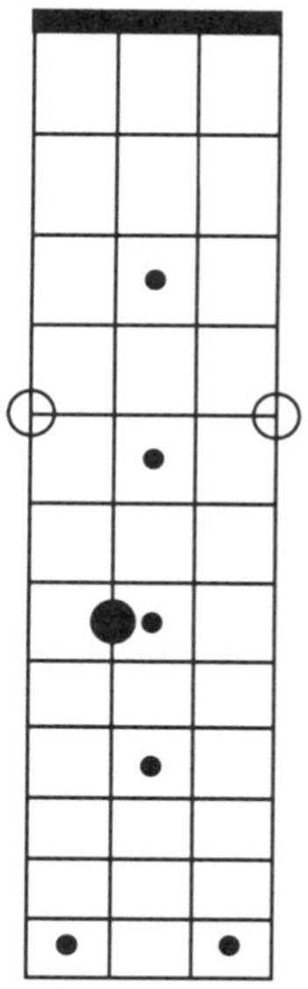

E7

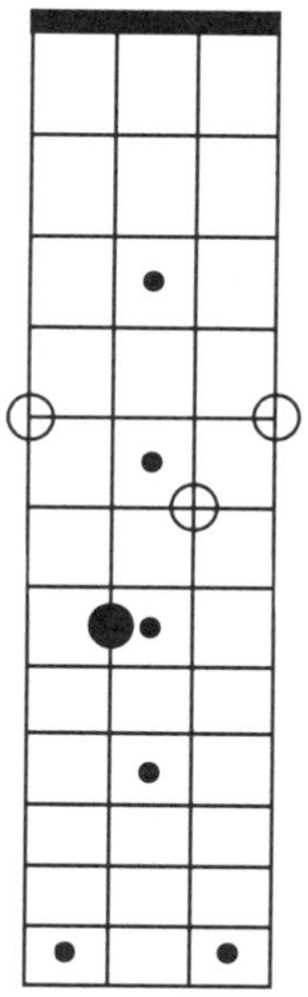

Em

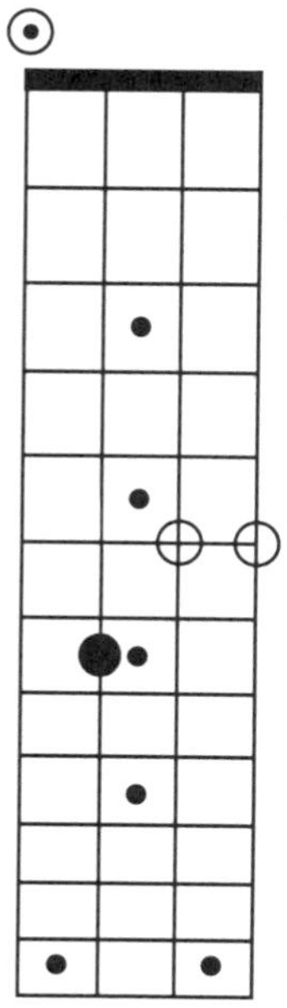

Em11

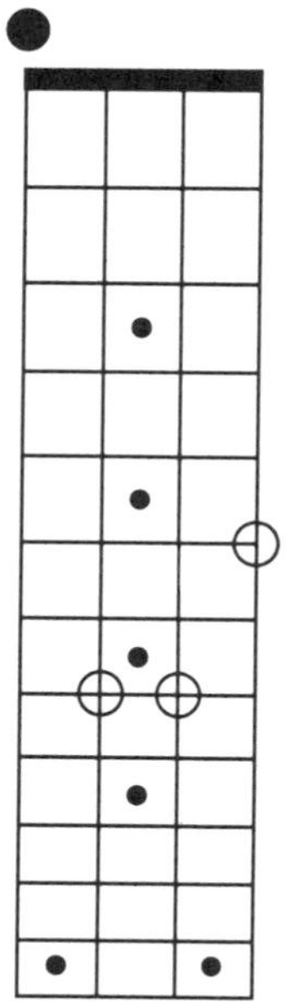

A

A

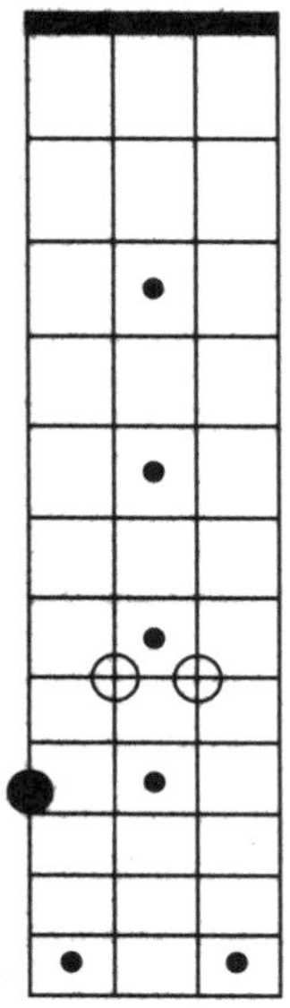

C♯ E A
3 5 1

A

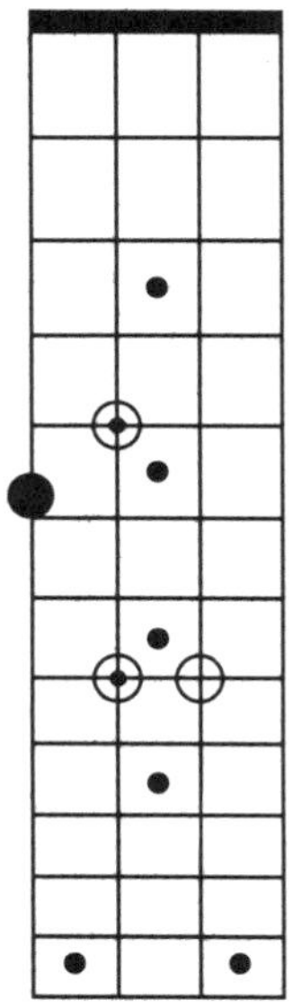

A C♯ A
1 3 1
or
E
5

A^7

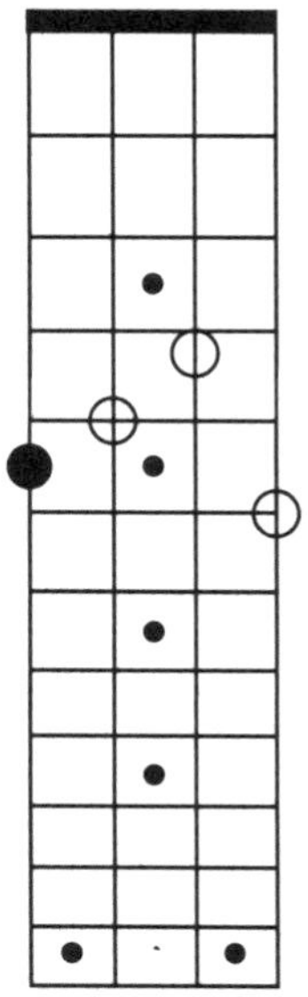

A C♯ A G
1 3 1 ♭7

Am

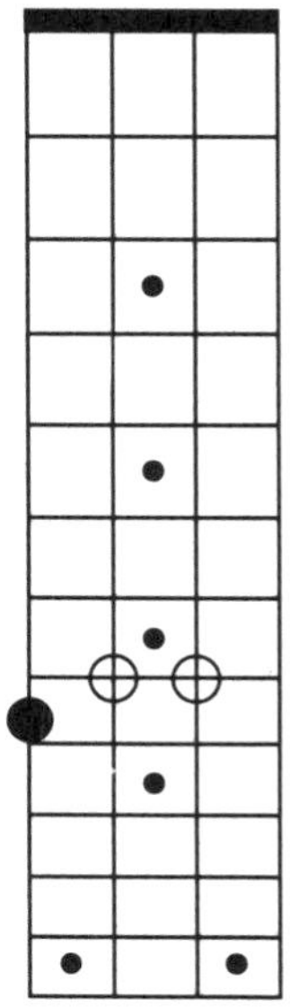

C E A
♭3 5 1

$A^{(\frac{6}{9})}$

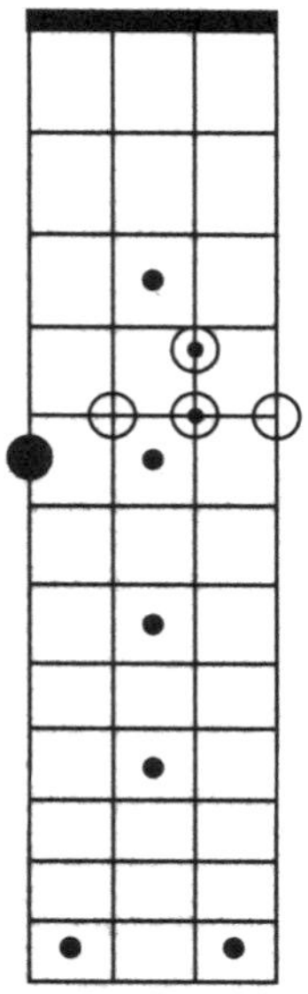

A C♯ F♯ B
1 3 6 9
or
A
1

A^{11}

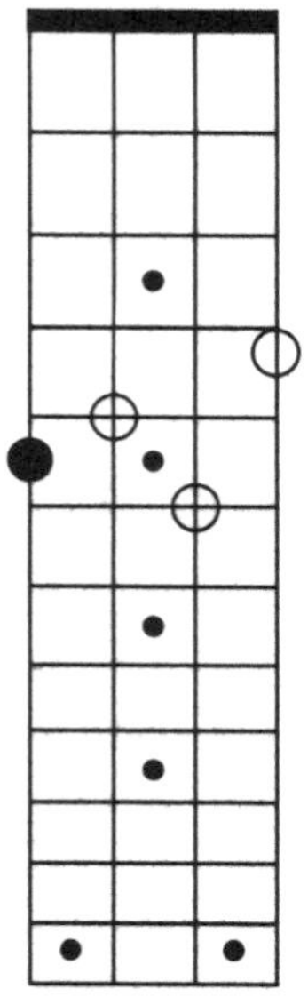

A C♯ D D
1 3 11 11

$A^{7(11)}$

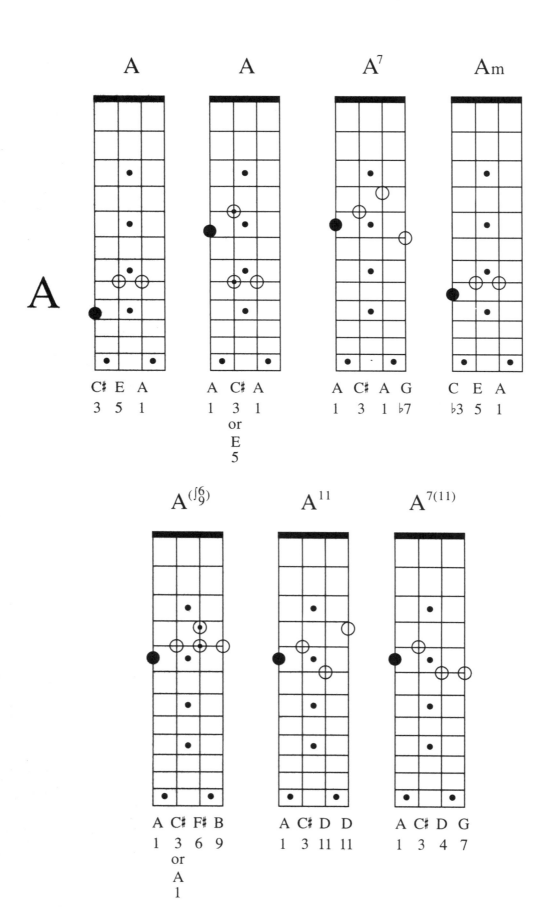

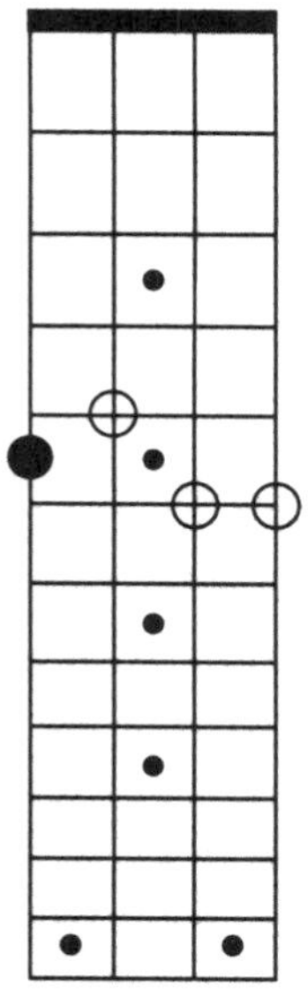

A C♯ D G
1 3 4 7

CHORD VOICING

We know already that in our basic tuning of perfect 4ths we have a semi-chromatic instrument with a set number of major and minor type keys available. The inherent keys and natural voice leading that comes about are of substantial consideration in applying chord voicing to harmonics.

The key of D major gives us a nice, neat package for chords and possibilities for voicings. Figure 21 makes this package quick and easy to visualize. Notice that the same chord form can be used for the entire progression because each voicing is modally related to the key of D.

Figure 21

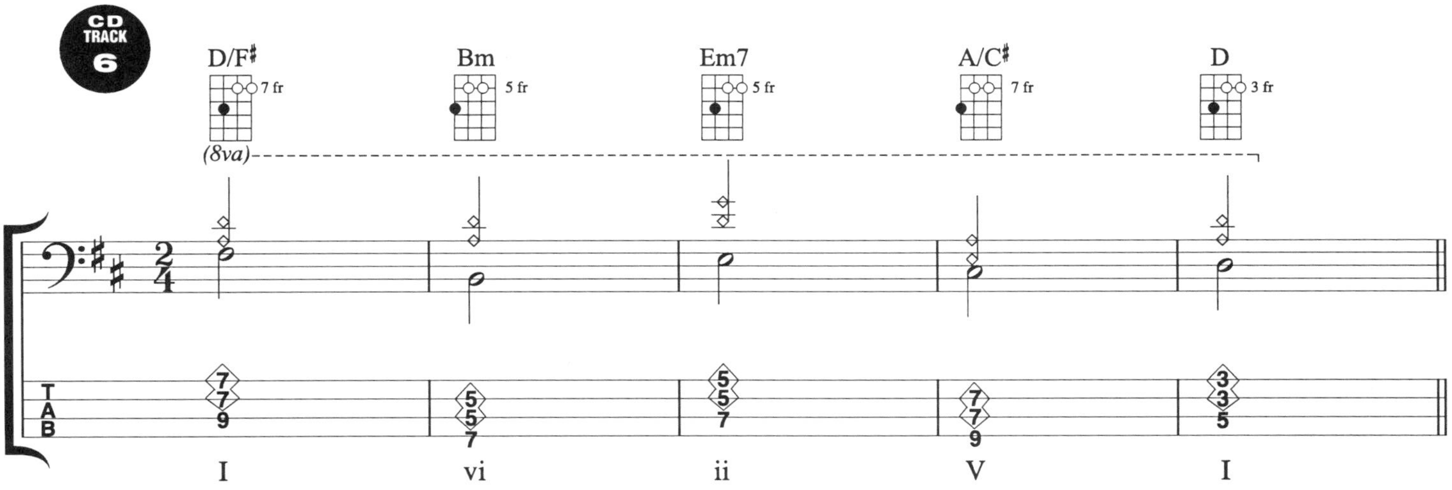

In each measure there is a chord written out in note form and in chord diagram. **Again, take special notice of the single chord fingering pattern used for each chord in the progression.**

Figure 22

CD TRACK 7

The studies contained in Figures 22, 23, and 24 demonstrate the inherent voicings found when using bass harmonics.

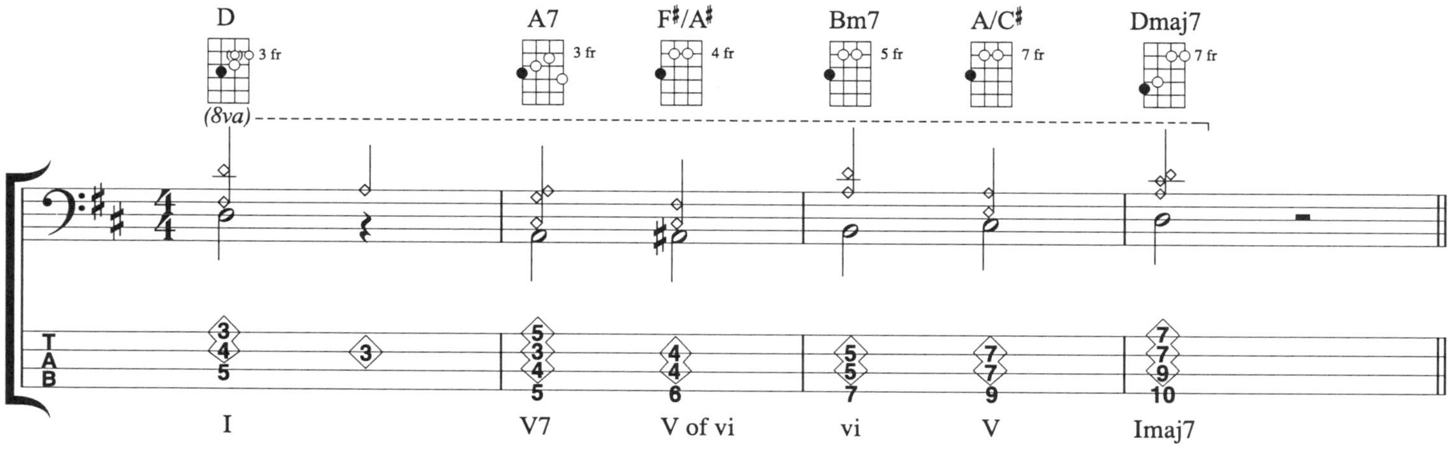

Figure 23

CD TRACK 8

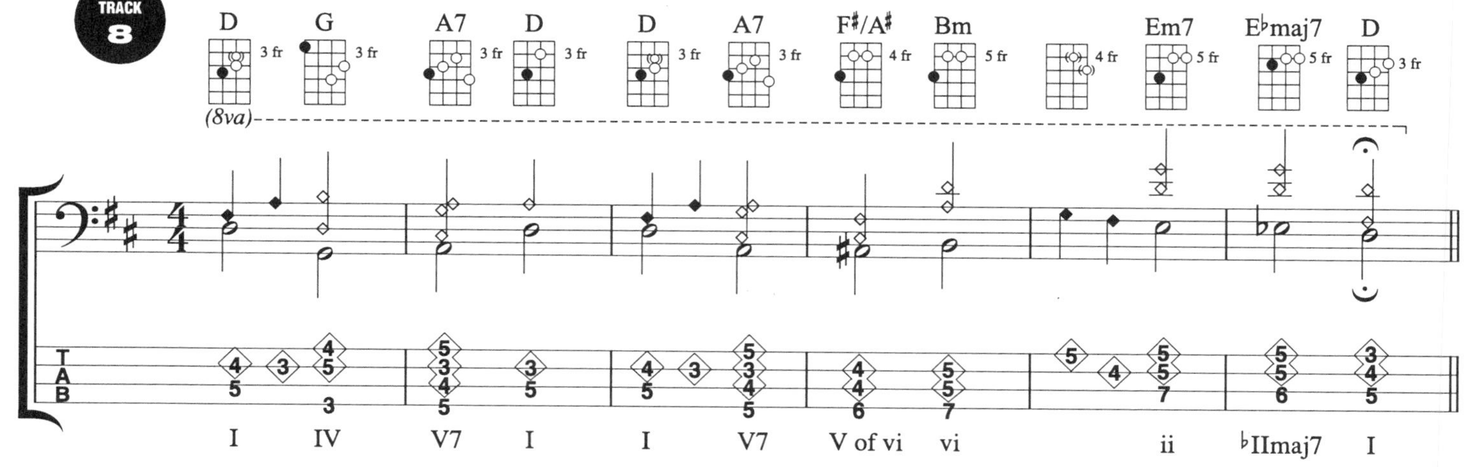

Figure 24

CD TRACK 9

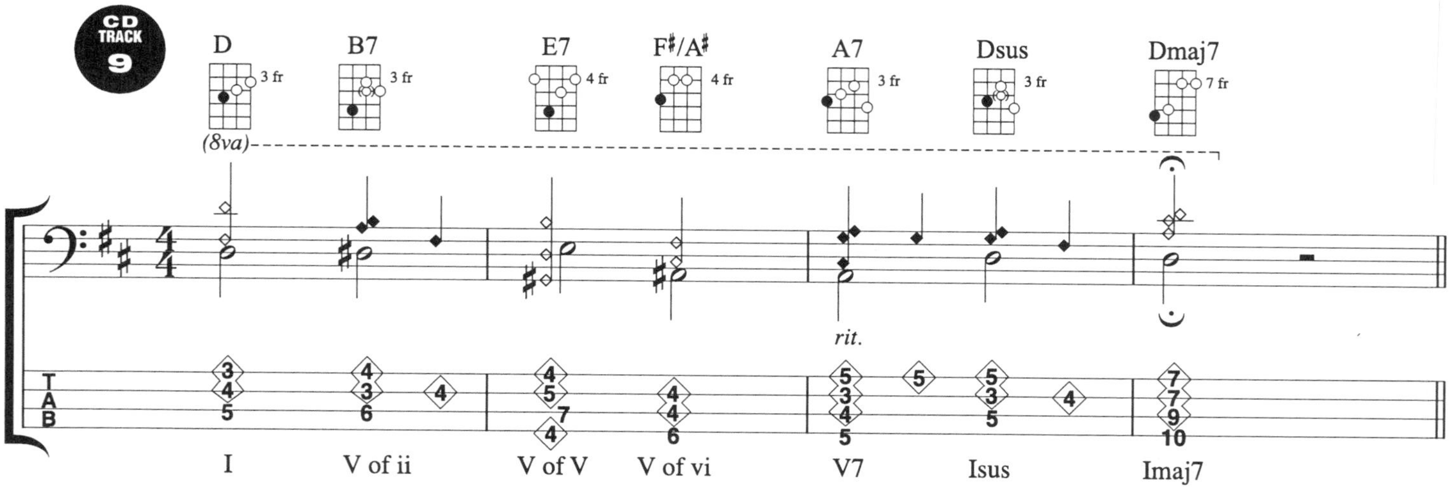

Figure 25

CD TRACK 10

It is necessary to keep in mind that **it takes at least three notes to state a tonal center.** You are then forced to begin looking for the best compromise toward establishing this. (See Figure 25)

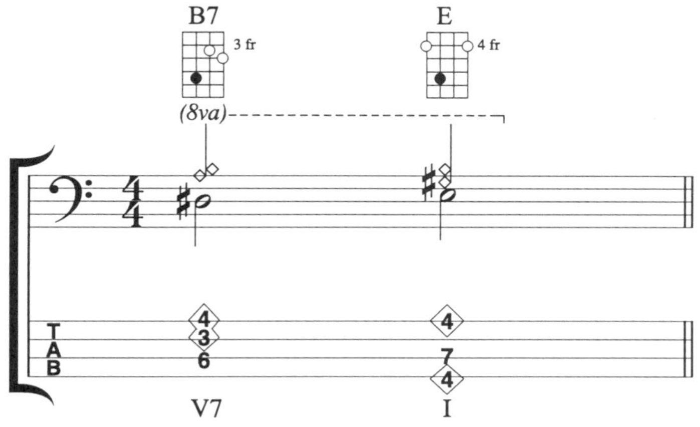

In the above example, the dominant 7 chord contains only three notes. The 5th is missing, but this chord does include the tri-tone—the interval that provides the essential pull toward the I chord. This is the type of process that works to establish a tonal center when you have missing notes.

You can use this same approach as you move toward the flat keys. Use the chord voicings from the above studies as foundations for your own compositions. As long as you choose generally accepted root movements, the naturally occurring chord voicing will flow smoothly together in whatever progression you choose. These chord voicings are unique to bass harmonics.

CHAPTER 4: OPEN TUNINGS

Open tunings are a good resource when trying to overcome the shortcomings of missing chord and scale tones from standard tuning of perfect 4ths. Look at what happens when we employ different intervals between strings (what you gain and what you lose) in the following example tunings. Regardless of the tuning, node points are always in the same location on the string.

Figure 26 shows the available harmonics with the G string brought down a 1/2 step to F♯. This tuning creates a major 3rd (rather than a perfect 4th) between 1st string (F♯) and the 2nd string (D). Since the 4th, 3rd, and 2nd strings remain unchanged, you keep some of your familiar territory, as well as netting the B♭ or A♯ which is normally missing. In this situation you are able to create a major triad with a single finger by barring straight across anywhere along the neck where harmonics are located.

Figure 26

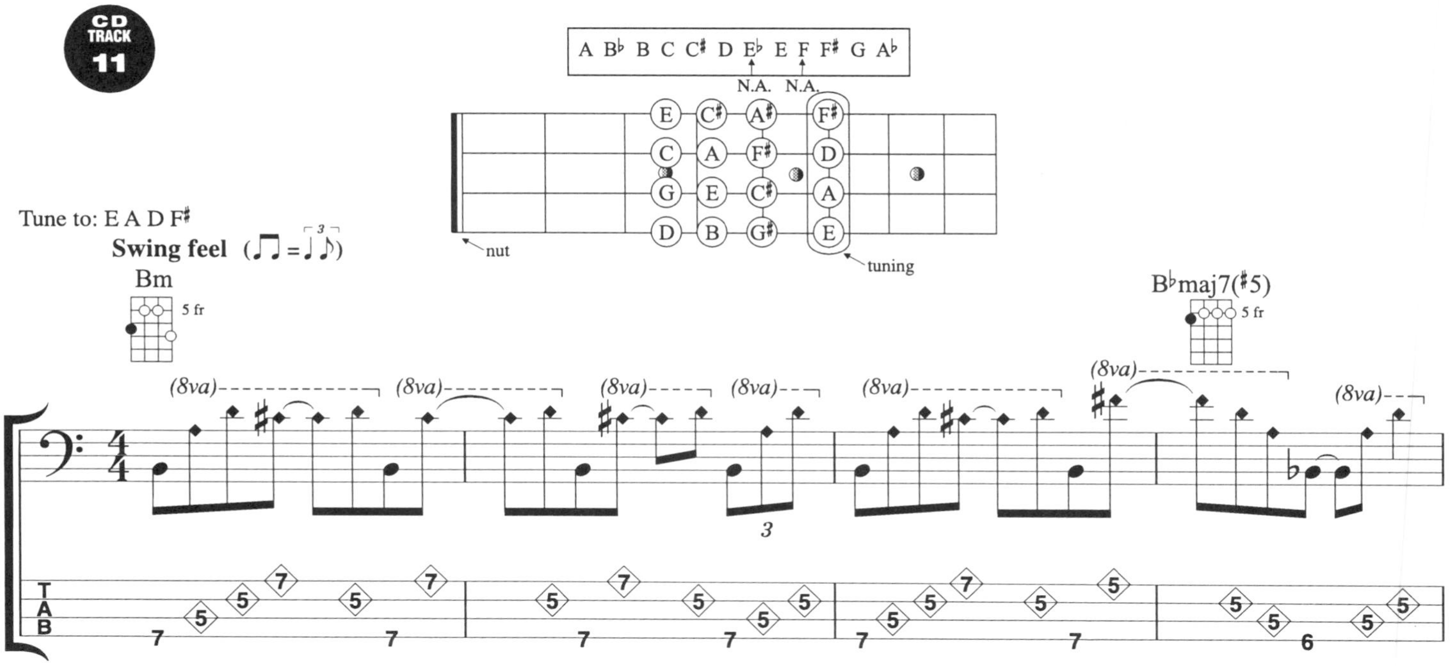

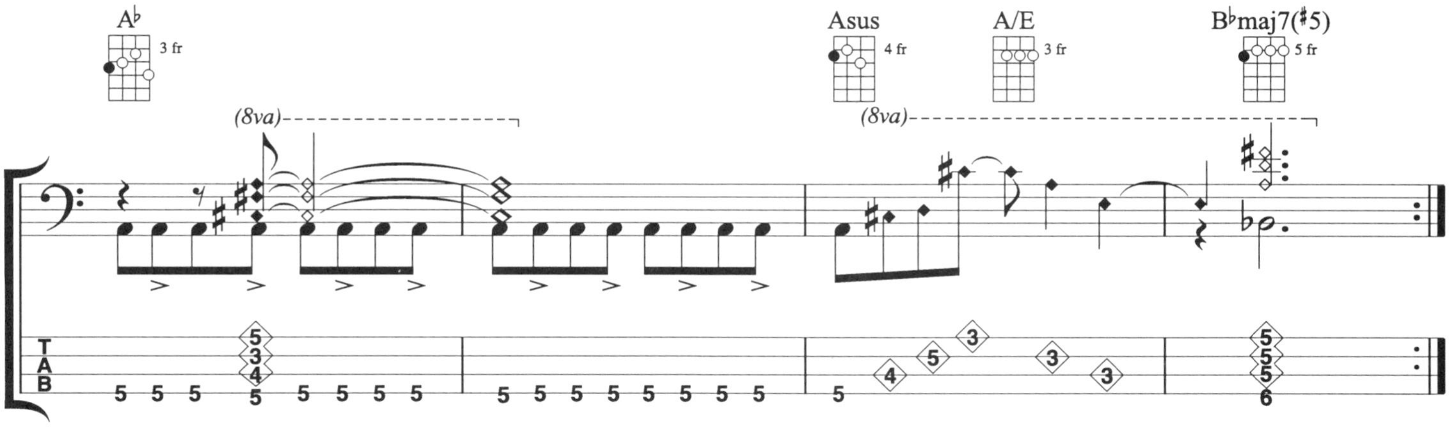

The more you alter the straight tuning of perfect 4ths, the farther away you go from your familiar territory, so let's look at a tuning where we do just that. Tune the strings to D A E G♯. In this tuning you are able to apply the same chord forms (or patterns) to achieve different results in chord type.

Figure 27

CD TRACK 12

When plucking harmonics, you may notice a difference in the way the string responds in both feel and sound. This difference is due to the uneven tension between strings.

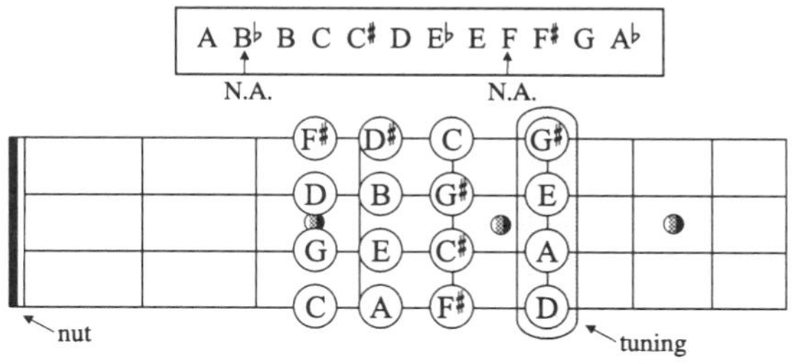

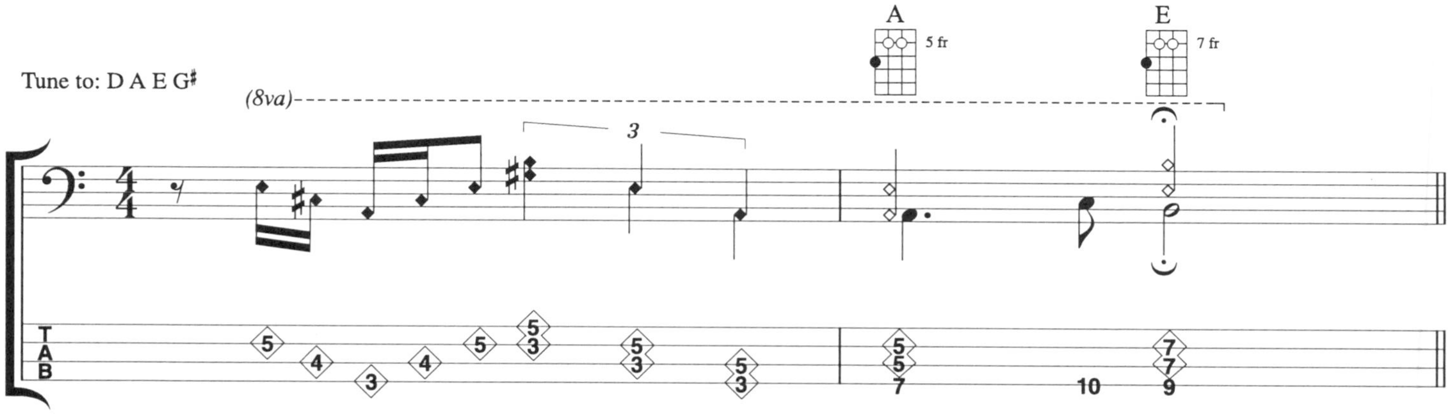

Figure 28

CD TRACK 13

Figure 28 is a musical example using a tuning of perfect 5ths. This demonstrates an interesting set of inherent chord voicings and scale possibilities.

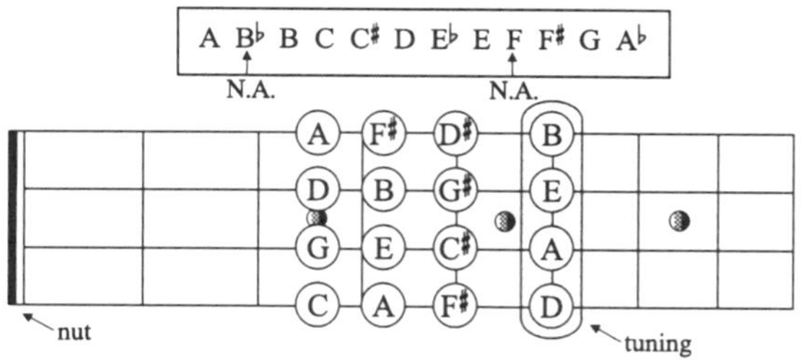

Tuning each string exactly 1/2 step higher completely shifts the inherent key structure from D to E♭, which is useful for playing with instruments whose inherent keys are flat (i.e., trumpet, alto sax). Transpose the music down a 1/2 step to facilitate a happy coexistence.

Points of interest regarding open tunings:

1) Some tunings will result in giving you repeat harmonics and narrowing down the field of possible notes. An example of this is a tuning of straight major 3rds. (See Figure 29.)

Figure 29

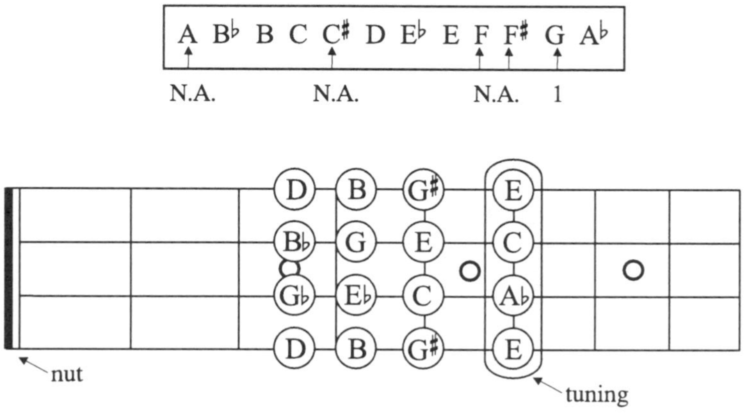

2) Being able to find letter names of harmonics is the same process as with standard tuning. You simply plug in the letter name of the string and spell all the notes on the string as you would spell a chord.

3) The gauge of the string and string tension each affect the overall harmonic response of a string. The strength of the bass neck determines how far the string can be stretched.

4) Each new tuning sets up a new inherent key.

5) Interacting with other musicians requires you to be comfortable with your own repertoire of tunings.

CHAPTER 5: DUAL NODE HARMONICS

A **dual node harmonic** is achieved by using two node points to create one sound. On one string you will touch two node points with your left hand. To accomplish this we use our first and fourth fingers.

The first diagram in Figure 30 shows the fourth finger directly above the 5th fret and the first finger to the bridge side of the 3rd fret. You must position your fingers very precisely. When done properly, this technique produces a very high, delicate sound. It will help if you pluck the string towards the bridge and have your rear pick up activated.

Before attempting the entire exercise, focus on playing the very first dual node harmonic correctly, and get a feel for the fingering and sound. In the end, what you will notice is the jump in pitch register and that by isolating the string length you can move the harmonic up and down the neck. The number of different dual node harmonics available is based on how far you can stretch your fingers.

Using dual node points provides clear access to higher ratio harmonics. Since higher ratio harmonics are in greater numbers and are closer together, they start to overlap and, in many cases, share the same space. By using two nodes you can absolutely define the ratio you need and uncover harmonics that are obscured.

One of the main advantages of using a second node point is that, because you can play a harmonic ratio in nearly any position along the string, other necessary stopped bass notes and chord or scale tones can be easier to reach. The chord diagrams below show the placement of the fingers in each measure. This figure also demonstrates how dual node points are just two node points of a single ratio. You can see that touching more than two node points of a single ratio is redundant and has no greater effect.

Figure 30

CD TRACK 14

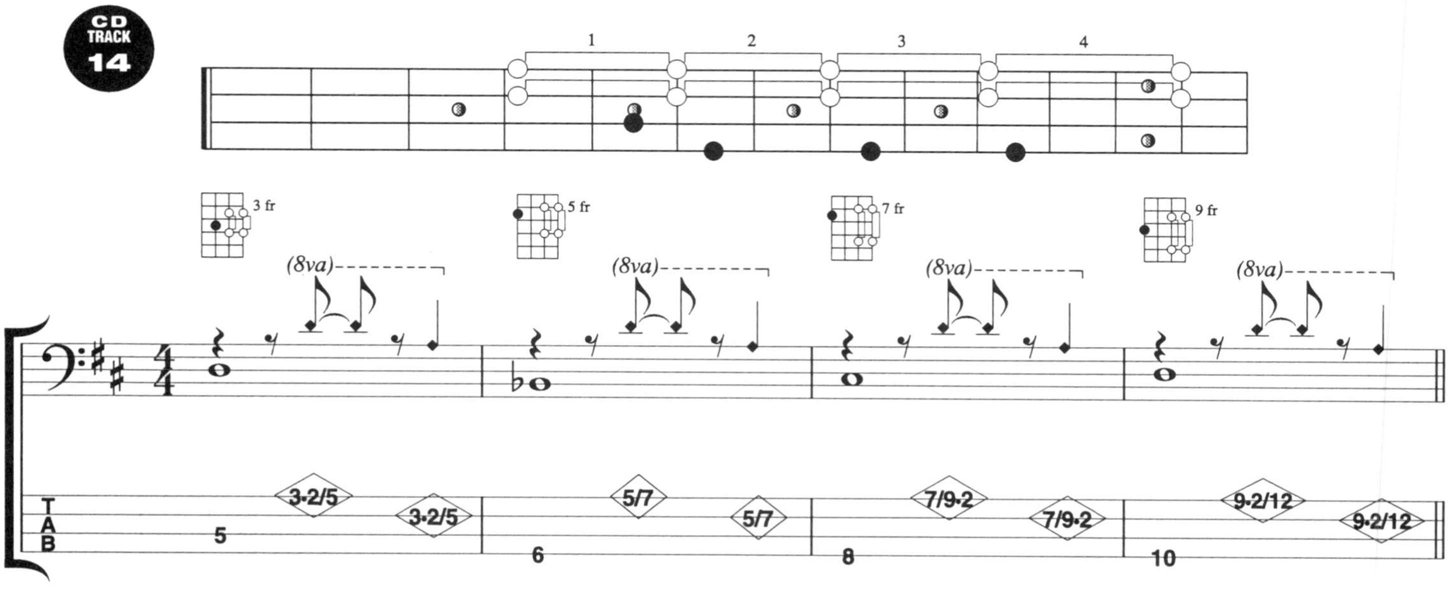

Dual node points provide a further “clearing away” of unwanted harmonics. Keep in mind that two left-hand fingers are occupied in playing each harmonic note instead of only one, so you use up available fingers, and the string must still have enough “speaking length” left to allow sufficient volume of the harmonic.

Finding the length of string necessary for a given ratio is simple. For example, let's say you need a 9:1 ratio on your G string. Measure from the nut (the first finger as shown in the photograph) to the first node (the fourth finger as shown in the photograph), and use this length to measure from the first node to the second, and so on, to identify each node position for the given ratio.

Figure 31

CHAPTER 6: FALSE HARMONICS

Techniques that require both hands to play harmonics fall under the general category of "false" harmonics. Using false harmonics is a great way to expand the note selection available to you as harmonics. False harmonics, however, are not a cure-all because of the differences in tonal quality and the fact that the technique occupies so many of your fingers.

A false harmonic rings from a stopped note rather than from the nut. By stopping a note, you change the speaking length of the string and, therefore, set up a new harmonic structure. (See Figure 32.)

Figure 32

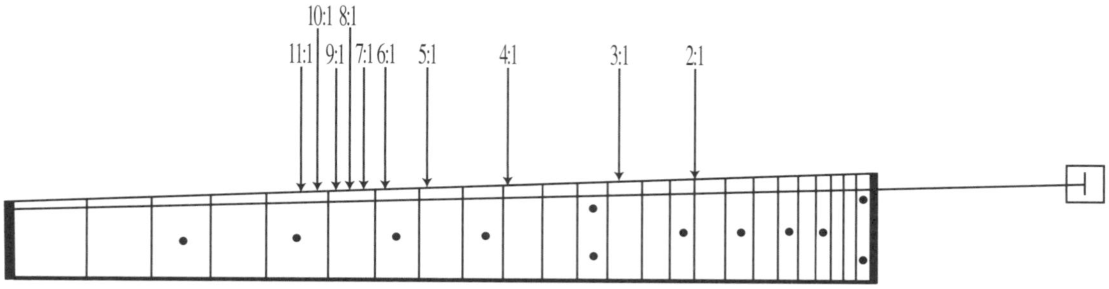

LEFT HAND

The first of several techniques for playing false harmonics is with just the left hand. (See Figure 33.)

Figure 33

CD TRACK 15

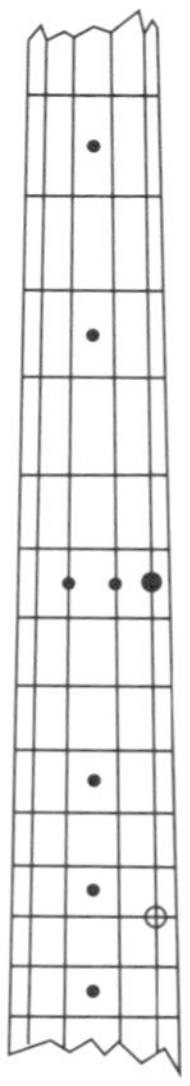

Figure 33 shows the left hand stopping G (12th fret) with the first finger and the fourth finger reaching for the 4:1 ratio (at the 17th fret.) The number of harmonic notes you can reach is dependent upon the size and dexterity of your hand. When you are really stuck for a harmonic that's not available, many times you can solve the problem through this particular false harmonic technique.

RIGHT HAND

Another technique for playing false harmonics takes advantage of harmonic ratios from the bridge side of the string. The first and second fingers of the right hand pluck the string while the side of the right-hand thumb lightly touches the desired ratio. The left hand determines the string length through the use of stopped notes. (See Figure 34.)

Figure 34

CD TRACK 16

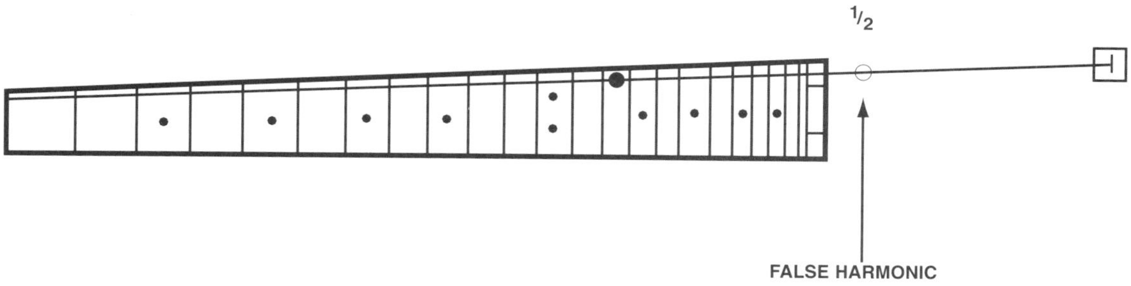

Figure 35

CD TRACK 17

For a warm, bell-like sound using false harmonics, track the 2:1 ratio for each stopped note, again using the side of the right thumb. This technique involves visually judging the halfway point between the stopped note and the bridge.

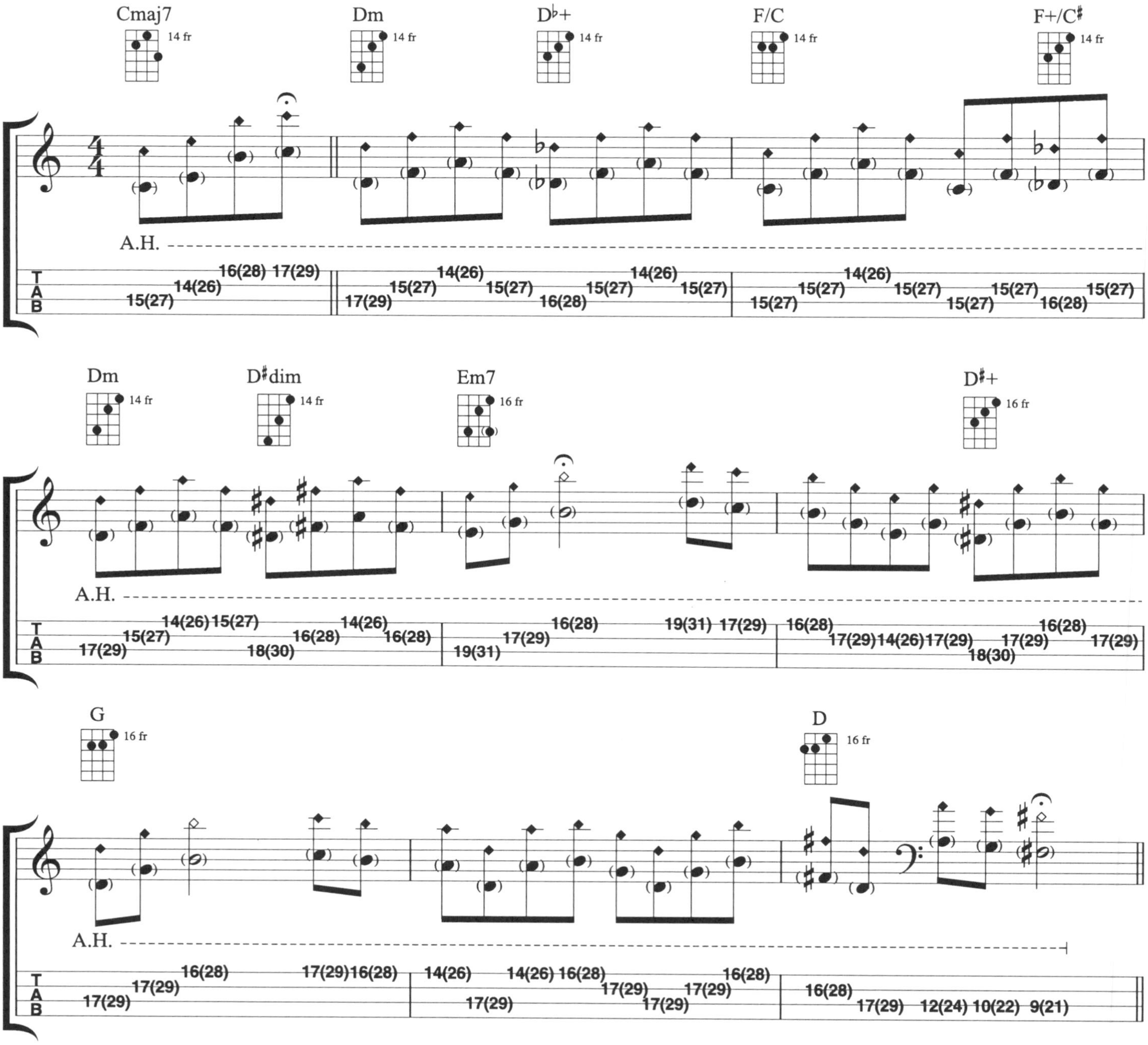

Figure 36

CD TRACK 18

In Figure 36, experiment with different ratios through the use of two variations of right-hand technique. The first way is to use the 8:1 tracking technique. You will hear the 2:1 ratio of every note you are playing (8:1 = 3 octaves higher). To hear which ratios occur randomly, leave your thumb in the same position while your left hand moves in the pattern. The result is a piercing, angular, squawking sound.

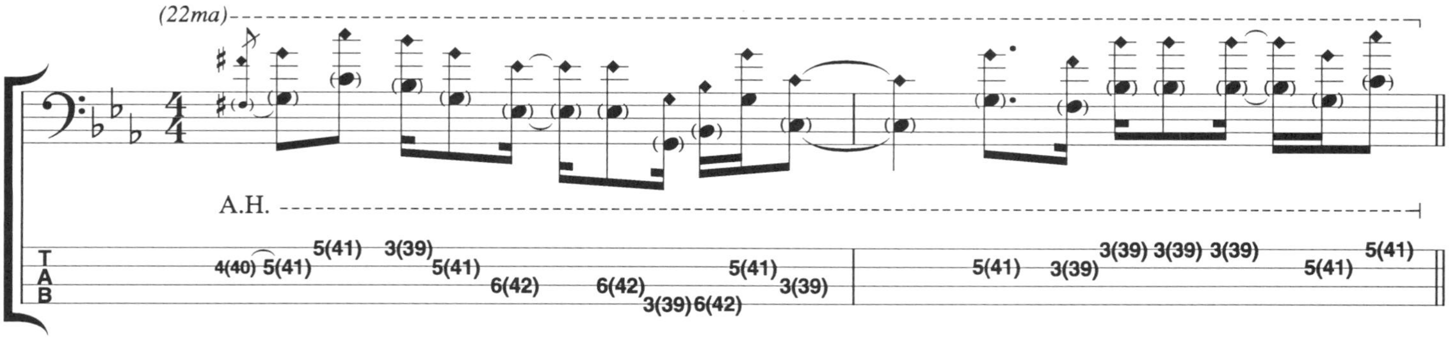

Figure 37

CD TRACK 19

Another possibility: Figure 37 again uses the 2:1 ratio, but instead of lightly touching the ratio with your right thumb, smack it with either your right thumb for a harsher, distorted bell sound, or with the tips of your fingers for a light, sharp bell sound. Try both.

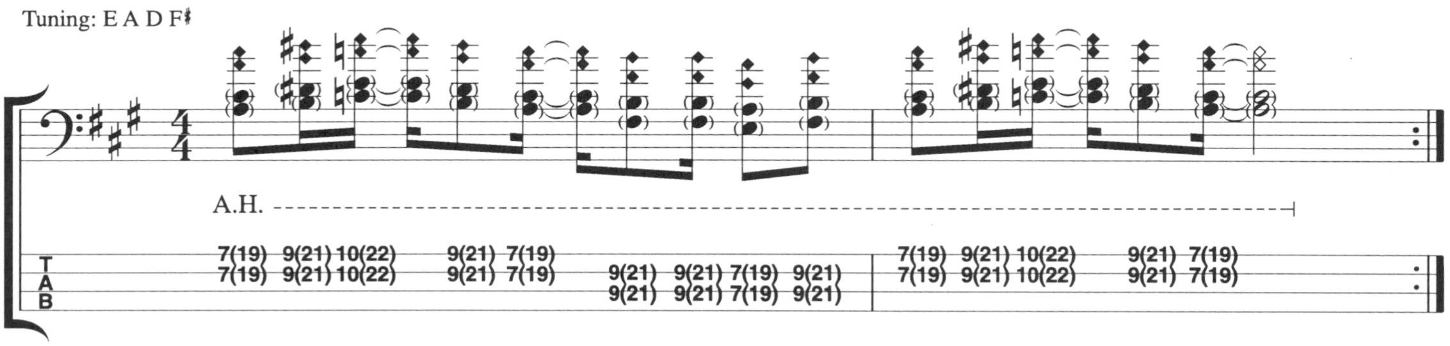

REACHING

Reaching for false harmonics allows you to play harmonics you would not normally be able to get using open strings. Figure 38 demonstrates an E major 7 chord.

Figure 38

CD TRACK 20

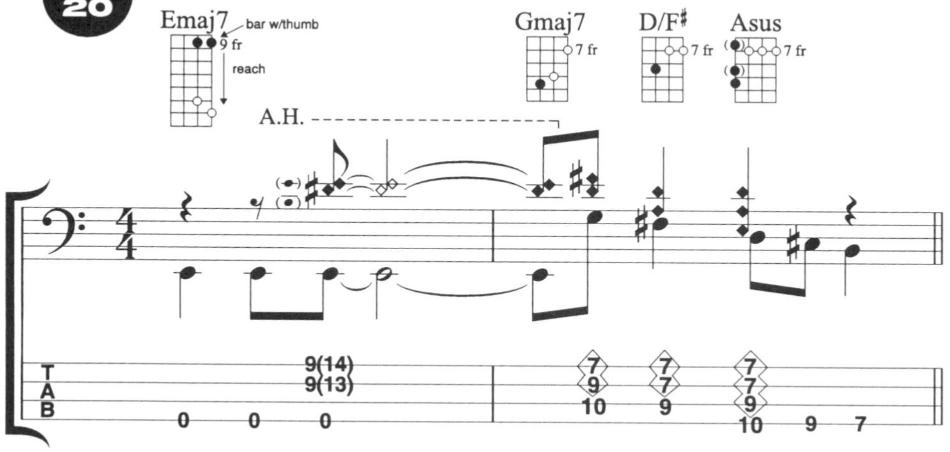

SLIDING HARMONICS

In order to accomplish sliding, push into the node points and then down into the fingerboard; next slide either up or down. This action changes the speaking length of the string and is especially useful in resolving suspensions or in finding needed chord or scale tones. The technique works for fretted and fretless instruments, but is smoother on fretless. (See Figure 39.)

Figure 39

CD TRACK 21

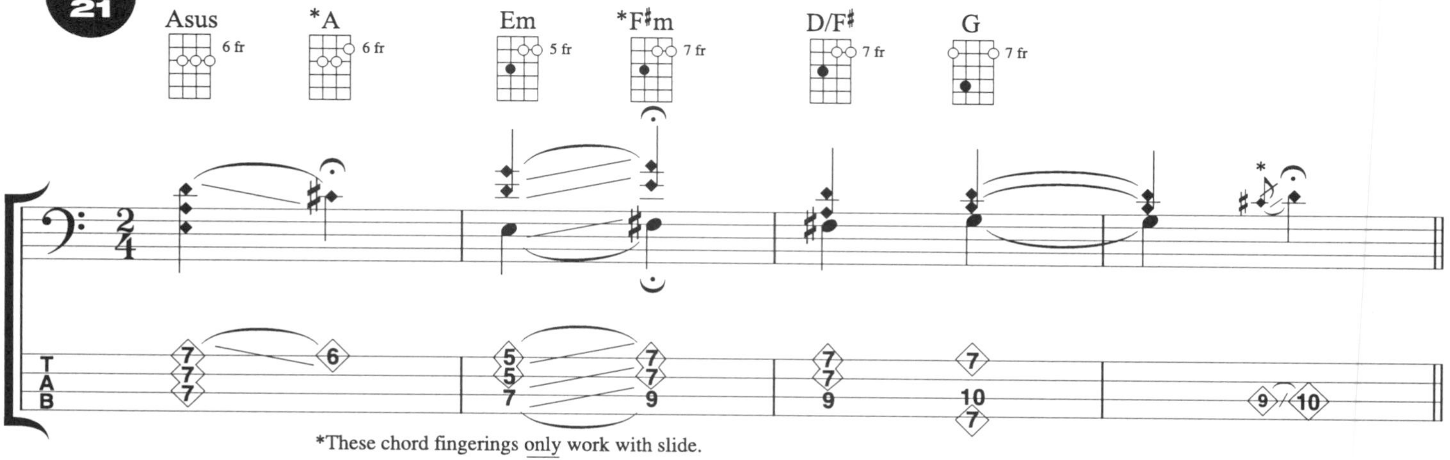

*These chord fingerings only work with slide.

CONCLUSION

This book was designed to be used as a permanent reference for incorporating bass harmonics into your bass playing vocabulary. Apply what you learn soon. Don't wait. Find out where bass harmonics fit into your style. To what extent you employ the subtle nuances that harmonics provide depends on your personal style as well as the style of music you apply them to. Remember, no matter where you pluck, don't be chicken to try.

GLOSSARY

ANTINODE: A vibrating string at its point of farthest excursion.

CHORD VOICING: The arrangement of voices within a chord vertically, and the selection of chord tones to be used.

CHROMATIC SCALE: A 12-note scale including all notes by consecutive 1/2-steps within an octave.

DIATONIC: Any eight musical notes in consecutive order (i.e., C D E F G A B C) that state a key or tonal center.

DUAL NODE POINTS: Two node points used to achieve a single harmonic ratio.

FALSE HARMONICS: A harmonic that rings from a stopped note rather than from the open string at the nut.

FREQUENCY: The number of cycles per unit time (i.e., cycles per second).

FUNDAMENTAL: The basic pitch of a musical note.

HARMONIC: The bell-like tone produced by lightly touching the string at one of its node points, thereby sounding one of the tones in that note's overtone series.

HIGHER RATIO HARMONICS: Harmonic ratios at or above the 8:1 ratio.

INVERSION: Chords with a bass note other than the root—usually the 3rd, 5th, or 7th.

MODE: Any diatonic scale (C to C, D to D, E to E, etc.).

NODE POINT: A place where there is no sound, and the pivotal point of a vibrating string. This is where the string must be touched to "sound" a harmonic.

OPEN TUNING: Tunings other than the standard tuning of E A D G.

TRACKING: Used with the false harmonic technique to produce a consistent single ratio.